IGHTING

# FLOOR FIGHTING

## Stompings, Maimings, and Other Things to Avoid When a Fight Goes to the Ground

Marc "Animal" MacYoung

Paladin Press
Boulder, Colorado

**Also by Marc "Animal" MacYoung:**

Barroom Brawling (video, with Peyton Quinn)
Cheap Shots, Ambushes, and Other Lessons
Down but Not Out (video)
Fists, Wits, and a Wicked Right
Knives, Knife Fighting, and Related Hassles
Pool Cues, Beer Bottles, and Baseball Bats
Professional's Guide to Ending Violence Quickly
Safe in the City (with Chris Pfouts)
Safe in the Street (video)
Street E&E
Surviving a Street Knife Fight (video)
Taking It to the Street
Violence, Blunders, and Fractured Jaws
Winning a Street Knife Fight (video)

*Floor Fighting: Stompings, Maimings, and Other Things
to Avoid When a Fight Goes to the Ground*
by Marc "Animal" MacYoung

Copyright © 1993 by Marc "Animal" MacYoung
ISBN 10: 0-87364-716-5
ISBN 13: 978-0-87364-716-8
Printed in the United States of America

Published by Paladin Press, a division of
Paladin Enterprises, Inc.
Gunbarrel Tech Center
7077 Winchester Circle
Boulder, Colorado 80301 USA
+1.303.443.7250

Direct inquiries and/or orders to the above address.

PALADIN, PALADIN PRESS, and the "horse head" design
are trademarks belonging to Paladin Enterprises and
registered in United States Patent and Trademark Office.

Visit our Web site at www.paladin-press.com

# CONTENTS

# WARNING

Some of the techniques and drills depicted in this book are extremely dangerous. It is not the intent of the author, publisher, or distributors of this book to encourage readers to attempt any of these techniques and drills without proper professional supervision and training. Attempting to do so can result in severe injury or death. Do not attempt any of these techniques or drills without the supervision of a certified instructor.

The author, publisher, and distributors of this book disclaim any liability from any damage or injuries of any type that a reader or user of information contained within this book may encounter from the use of said information. This book is for information purposes only.

# INTRODUCTION

"Cry 'Havoc!' and let slip the dogs of war!"
—William Shakespeare, *Julius Caesar*

I decided it was time to intervene when one of the hookers started pounding the other's head against the asphalt of Sunset Boulevard. I walked out of work and crossed the parking lot into the street. Horns were blaring at the two women, whose sudden brawl had brought all traffic on the boulevard to a screeching halt. As I stepped into the street from the north side, the pimp of one of the girls stepped into the street from the south. We looked at each other levelly for a moment and nodded. A message of the street passed between us. It wasn't between him and me; we were just there to break it up. The fight between the women was over. Everyone knew who had won; it was now time to stop it before somebody got seriously hurt.

The obvious winner was sitting on the other's chest and had two handfuls of hair, by which means she was repeatedly slamming the back of the loser's head into the asphalt. The loser was trying desperately to gouge out her assailant's

eyes with her long acrylic fingernails. They go down hard in
Hollywood.

The pimp grabbed his girl by the hair and shoulder and
dragged her off her victim. As I expected, the woman whose
head had been jackhammering the asphalt tried to rear up
and continue the fight.

I grabbed her by her tacky rabbit fur jacket and dragged
her back. She attempted a long kick at her attacker that
missed as I dragged her back onto her feet. Suddenly, she
lunged at her attacker. I caught her by the waist and snapped
my head back as she tried to elbow me in the face. Her
attempt to break my jaw was only half-hearted, as she was
mostly interested in freeing herself and resuming the fight.
When you break up fights, you have to expect to have a few
shots thrown at you for interrupting the fun.

I snarled in her ear, "Run, the cops!" Sure enough, down
the street a siren could be heard. By its pitch I could tell it
was an ambulance rather than a police car. Cops in
Hollywood don't really bother with fights between street
people until weapons come into play; then it's mostly to pick
up the pieces. Besides, the fight hadn't lasted long enough for
the call to go through the system and have a car respond.
Nonetheless, the ploy had the desired effect. The hooker's
attention flickered away from her opponent and toward me.
Her face was a mass of blood and fury. She didn't know who
I was, but she knew what a siren meant. Hookers hate jail
time—money not being made, lack of drugs, and someone
moving into their territory all make being in jail a hassle. Of
all the street people, hookers seem to hate doing jail time the
most. She turned quickly and ran up the street.

When I returned to the shop, my boss looked at me and
said, "You're crazy! They could have had knives!" I thought
about it for a second as I washed the blood off my hands.

"Nah. If they did, they would have been using them on
each other already . . ."

That most fights end up on the ground was no surprise to
me. Unlike many people, I learned how to wrestle and fight

on the floor at an early age. The fact that my older brother was on the wrestling team had a whole lot to do with my learning very early about what to do on the ground. His training, when combined with fierce sibling rivalry, led to fights that were designed to maim. As you might guess, this meant that I had a lot of practice fighting on the ground.

As a now retired streetfighter, I am evilly entertained by the three greatest lies in the world: 1) I won't cum in your mouth; 2) the check is in the mail; and 3) we don't get knocked down in fights.

The last one is only applicable if you study the martial arts. Most martial art forms require their practitioners to spend inordinate amounts of time practicing on their feet but zippo time on floor work. Even systems that promote throws and locks most of the time go to pieces when they're proponents are dragged to the ground with their victim.

It's not that I'd call anyone a prima donna or anything (yeah, right, sure!), but the American martial arts world had its panties in a wad for a very long time over a certain incident that occurred regarding William Cheung, the grand master of wing chun kung fu and a student of another master by the name of Ling Ti (?). If you peer through all the smoke and dust that was kicked up, you'll see a major weakness of most martial arts training.

William Cheung had issued the pro forma challenge that he would fight anyone to prove the effectiveness of his system. In professional American martial arts, these sort of challenges are routinely issued. More importantly, except for the Gracie family and a few like them, these challenges are routinely ignored in lieu of the much safer name-calling bouts that are egged on, if not actively promoted, by the martial arts magazines.[1]

Rumor has it that there had been long-standing attitudes between these two masters. Up to this point, however, it had just looked like one of those woofing contests that professional martial artists so love to get into. During a seminar of Master Cheung's, this student of Ling Ti walks in and basi-

3

cally says, "Let's go for it." The response was, "No, no, not now. We'll set it up for later." "Nope, it's party time!" Right then and there, the guy attacks the grand master of wing chun. And the way that he beat the grand master of wing chun was that he basically tackled him. Once he had him down on the ground, it was a one-way conversation.

The uproar was incredible in the martial arts world. For about a year and a half, you couldn't open up a martial art rag without running into something about it. The complaints were basically threefold: 1) the guy was rude and didn't follow proper form for a challenge match (like I used to get formal challenges in bars all the time—sheesh!); 2) he had disrespected a master; and 3) (get this) he hadn't fought fair. While my opinion of the first two varies between "I could give a rat's ass" and "yeah, well okay," the third point is enough to set me giggling.

In case you haven't noticed, there is something that a Hollywood hooker, a martial arts grand master, and myself all have in common: we've all ended up on the ground in real fights. How well we did there depended on what we knew about floor fighting.

There are three main ways that you can end up on the floor during a fight: 1) you slip; 2) you're thrown, tripped, shoved, or knocked over; and 3), the most common, somebody decides to close and you both go down. In other words, you got tackled.

In situations one and two, you're on the ground and your opponent is still standing. This is referred to as a categorically bad situation. While certain fighting forms are designed to fight from the ground or low positions, they are rare and obscure. [2] The bad news is there are a number of forms that rely on knocking you off balance or throwing you. Oddly enough, what's taught in America doesn't deal with what should be done if you decide to take them with you. They're great at throwing you, but they get confused if they end up on the ground, too.

A major problem is that the throwing forms often don't

teach you to get up fast enough. If you're thrown in aikido or judo, you slap the mat when you fall. That resounding slap shows that your opponent has done a good throw (the same trick is used in TV wrestling). In the dojo, your partner stops and you get up and do it over again. This doesn't teach a number of critical points. These are: 1) get up immediately, and, if possible, 2) add energy to your fall so you can spring up out of range. In judo competitions, you lose points if you throw someone and he "falls badly." In a streetfight, you want your opponent to fall badly. An entirely different set of rules apply in a brawl. You have to learn to compensate for the new rules.

The real problem with being on the ground with your opponent still standing is that, unlike in a dojo, your attacker isn't going to stop. Either he is going to start kicking you (possibly with the help of his friends) or he's likely to pick up a chair and try to swat you like a bug. Neither "stompings" or stopping furniture with your body is a fun event.

All of those possibilities, however, are still not as common as number three above. A number of fights start with one guy tackling the other guy. This can happen in a variety of ways. Someone says something and the other guy muckles onto him and they both go down in a flurry of arms and legs. (Someone who starts a fight like this is either a wrestler or an untrained fighter. In the latter case, there probably won't be much damage done. If it is the former, it could get ugly real quick.)

Another way you can end up on the ground is when you and someone else are merrily exchanging punches and somehow you close and go down ass over tea kettle. This happens a lot—nobody's winning or losing yet, you just both get tangled up and end up on the floor.

Probably the most common way to end up on the ground occurs in places where "punch outs" are still happening. I'm talking in nearly any high school and especially college bars. This is when someone begins to lose the fight and grabs onto his opponent as a last-ditch effort. This is officially to pin his attacker's arms, but it usually results in everyone ending up ass over elbow. This often takes down a few spectators to boot.[3]

In this book, I'm going to cover the three aspects of floor fighting: you down/him up, both down, and him down/you up. Believe it or not, in all three cases, who walks away from a floor fight often depends on what was done before you hit the ground. This is a combination of minimizing your damage and maximizing his. A whole lot of it has to do with not only surviving the fist impact but using the situation to your advantage. While a number of people are beaten to death in this country every year, a thunderin' herd of those deaths occur when someone slams his head against the concrete when he falls. We're going to cover that, too.

Now I gotta tell you, a whole lot of my time in other books has been devoted to figuring out ways to avoid fights. I still believe in Sun Tzu's concept of "Battleless Victory," or winning without having to strike a blow. But I've pretty much shot my wad on avoiding violence. It's now time to deal with the bone-breaking, ball-cracking, eye-gouging nastiness that I used to get through the streets of Los Angeles. My preference would be for you to use the avoidance techniques and ideas that I have mentioned elsewhere.[4] However, if it looks like you have no choice but to fight, "better him than you."

## FOOTNOTES

[1] What generally happens is the masters sit back and send out their best and brightest to do their dirty work for them. Students from one school will wipe out students from another school at tournaments. Evidently, few hot-shot teachers want to risk blowing the reputation of how awesome their system is by getting personally stomped in grudge matches with someone from a competing system. If a student goes down in a tournament, it's one thing. If the head of a school or system gets plastered all over the wall, it sort of deflates the myth of how good the system is.

[2] There exists an Indonesian fighting form where people imme-

diately sit down. This is done because the area where it's from is usually 6 inches deep in mud. It's like fighting on ice, so they immediately drop down. Some of the more obscure Shao Lin forms fight from low down, too, but the applied effectiveness of these systems is somewhat doubtful.

[3] At a party, I once saw a couple of young bucks plow into the girl that they were fighting over. She wasn't amused about being fought over like a piece of property in the first place, but when they landed on top of her, she went apeshit. The fight had been civilized compared to what she did when she got up.

[4] Also, you're less likely to meet the cops if you try to avoid fights. The legal system in this country is so screwed up that, even if you were in the right, you can end up in some serious trouble. And even if you don't get arrested and thrown in jail, civil suits are majorly expensive and time-consuming.

# 1 THE BASICS

> *"Adventure is just a romantic name for trouble. It sounds swell when you write about it, but it's hell when you meet it face to face in a dark and lonely place."*
>
> —Louis L'Amour

Matthew and I had closed the distance and were gleefully hacking away at each other with 3-foot-long broadswords. It didn't matter that they were real steel swords because we were both in plate armor and chain mail. Contrary to popular opinion, a broadsword against full plate armor isn't much of a threat, so we were having a howlingly good time beating the hell out of each other. Blood did flow freely in these bouts, but lost fingers, cracked bones, and the occasional stab wound to a limb were the worst things to ruin our fun. Of course, only if your definition of a good time is trying earnestly to hack your friends up with archaic weapons could this be called fun.

Our swords locked, and I risked a punch to his face. The fact that I had a chain mail gauntlet and neither of us were wearing helmets made his preventing the blow from landing rather important. He rolled away from the punch and shoved me away. The direction that he shoved me was at odds with my stance integrity, so I fell over backward.

As I fell, I knew I had to do something quick or I'd be in some serious trouble. I shifted my body position and held my sword arm out so I wouldn't fall on my own sword. Neither Japanese or Roman, I. Instead, I turned my fall into a backward roll. The amount of dust a guy in armor doing back rolls can kick up is incredible. As I came up into a kneeling position, I peered through the dust to see Matthew charging me with a maniacal rictus of glee on his face. His charging me was not half as much of a concern as the fact that he had his sword over his head ready for a double-handed downward stroke. Even if I had had a helmet on, that would have been too much of a blow to take.

I threw myself into another back roll to buy myself distance. As I did, I began to bring my sword back into line. When I finished the second roll, my sword was up over my head in a double-handed grip at each end. The blow landed between my hands on the blade. While the impact nearly compacted my spine, his stroke didn't split my skull as he had intended it to. I figured since he had tried to cave my head in, I should have no reservations about trying to damage him right back. I shifted my grip to a double-handed swing and from a kneeling position tried to smash his left knee. Discretion being the better part of valor, he leaped back.

His momentary retreat gave me enough time to scramble back onto my feet. We charged each other again, and the battle resumed. Later, when we were trying to recover by pouring copious amounts of beer down our throats, the witnesses to the melee were in awe of this fancy move I had done. Someone asked me where I had learned it, and between chugs of beer, I muttered, "The 'oh shit' school!" It took the woman a moment to realize that it had been a purely reflexive move in an attempt to save my ass.

That little episode was probably the most spectacular bit

of floor work I've ever done. There have been other incidents, but none of them looked anywhere near as good. Others were more effective, but none of them would have Errol Flynn fans panting so nicely. Nonetheless, this incident exemplifies the four laws of surviving a trip to the floor.

1) Minimize the impact/damage of the fall.
2) Buy yourself distance from your attacker.
3) Regroup your defenses and, if possible, your offense.
4) GET UP IMMEDIATELY!

Look at the story again and see how each of these four criteria were met. Throughout this book, we are going to return to these four key laws, as they are critical to surviving a trip to the floor. We are now going to look at one and four and how they can work together.

As kids, my brother and I used to get into balls-to-the-wall wrestling matches with our stepfather. It was not uncommon for us to become airborne in these little tussles. Throws, flips, and tosses were common. Fortunately, one of the first things we learned was how to tumble to minimize the damage. Both my brother and I were slammed off walls, cabinets, and the couch more than once. Since this was seriously rough and tumble, it became vital to learn how to minimize the possibility of major damage. This ability to "tuck and roll" is key to minimizing the damage of a fall. (I should also point out that it has saved my life in car, bicycle, and motorcycle accidents, as well as in falls, leaps, drops, and collapsing buildings. It has more applications than just fighting.[1])

The secret to tumbling is to turn your body into a ball or a curve. The spot most likely to fill this job description is your back. If your body is held straight (or at rigid angles) when it hits the ground, all of the force is going to impact into you. If your body is curved or rounded before the impact, the energy is going to bleed off and you'll roll. Take a look at the illustration:

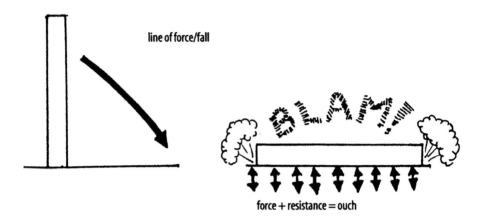

line of force/fall

force + resistance = ouch

Not a good situation, this. When sufficient resistance is met, the force of the falling body (mass x velocity) is transferred back into the body. This means the body absorbs the shock of its force being stopped. Face it, the ground is bigger than you. It can take the impact; you can't. Now let's look at another scenario with a different shape:

Ah-hah! What is he trying to tell me?! Could it be that a curve during a fall hurts less?! Could be, Buckwheat.

Remember, the number one law of making it out of a floor situation is to minimize the damage of the fall. Even if you slam into a

line of force/fall

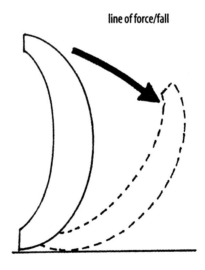

**new channeled force direction**

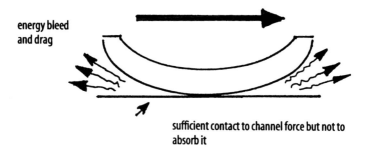

**energy bleed
and drag**

**sufficient contact to channel force but not to
absorb it**

**altered direction
of force**

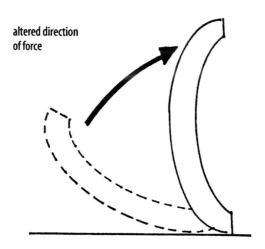

wall in the middle of a roll, you've bled off enough energy that the impact is going to be less than if you fell straight over or flew into the wall directly. I'd rather hit an unmoving wall doing a roll that's slowed me to 10 miles an hour than meet the same wall doing a head dive at 65.

I mentioned that the back is your best area for creating the curve you'll need to take a fall. That's true, but your arms, shoulders, and legs all play major parts in this movie, too. Let's take a look at the angles that work best for rolls.

13

When that ball of spaghetti is unravelled, it boils down to only three different angles: side to side, up and down, and diagonal, or, putting it in quasi-gymnastic terms, side rolls, forward/ backward rolls, and shoulder rolls.

I highly recommend that you go out and either take some classes at the local YMCA or gymnastics school, or pick up some books on gymnastics or movie stunt work to learn how to tumble correctly. It's called floor work in gymnastics. While I admit that I got to advanced gymnastics in high school, I'm not a teacher of gymnastics. I can only point out some things and recommend you practice tumbling under the tutelage of someone who is a better gymnast than me.

I also suggest you learn tumbling from a gymnast rather than an aikido or judo instructor. Tumbling is concerned not only with hitting the floor but using the energy to get back up again, while the training you get in martial arts classes is directed at falling either in "proper form" or "mat slapping" to show that you've fallen and it's time to stop.

Another place not to learn how to fall is from professional wrestling. Not only are these stunt falls onto a padded surface, but the fallee stays down there. Look what staying down there gets them (oh, besides a few grand a match). Even with stunt falls, you can get hurt. Also, watch how many times those moves are made to sound worse with a foot stomp or arm slap to the mat. In a real fight, the guy isn't going to stop just because you hit the ground. Law number four comes into play—get up quick.

I cannot begin to stress how important laws 1 and 4 are. In fact, I'm going to take this opportunity to point something out that really frosts my ass. My lady, Tracy, has a grandfather who teaches judo. Naturally, she was trained in judo. Well, she then decided to take aikido. One of her instructors got seriously anal about the fact that she was doing judo rolls rather than aikido rolls. They'd fall and slap the mat and the process would stop, then start over again. He was getting his panties in a wad about her landings being the wrong style. Not that they didn't work—they did—they were just the wrong style of fall. To hear him, you'd have thought that the world was going to end.

I, in the meantime, was sitting over in the corner biting my tongue, because a formal aikidoist or judoka would never dream of kicking someone in the face or breaking the guy's arm once he's on the floor. I would, but I'm a fucking barbarian; this is a martial *art!* (Of course, part of the reason I am a barbarian is I say fuck the art, get the job done. If I'm so inclined, when the guy is down I might just add a barstool to the process. Barbarous, but effective.)

Going back to tumbling, the way to do it effectively is to turn your body into a curve in the same direction that you're falling. This lessens the impact and begins to channel the energy into propulsion rather than impact. This works the same if you're going over backward, forward, or sideways. The same principle you're going to learn here also applies if the guy is going down with you. There are a number of important changes if you're about to hit the floor with company, but the basic premise of minimizing the damage through shifting your body remains the same.

## BACKWARD AND FORWARD ROLLS

Most people fear going over backward the most. In light of the way that most people do it, they have every right to be concerned. They end up either landing straight on their ass or first bounce off their ass then keel over and land flat on their backs. This also contributes to the whipping of the head that either knocks out or kills many people when they hit the ground. Failing to cave their skulls in, many people settle for hurting their back, dislocating their hip, cracking ribs, and my all-time favorite, breaking an arm while trying to catch themselves. Again, I'm not only talking about fighting but slipping in the shower, on ice, wet surfaces, etc. Take a look below at this and tell me if you've seen this very thing in your life.

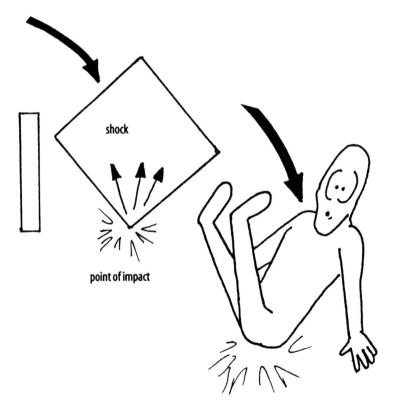

shock

point of impact

16

What is happening with the person is better described by the block and stick illustration next to him. The legs and pedestal are acting only as stands from which the body and block can fall. In short, all they are doing is acting as something to add height and speed to increase the impact. In both cases, the corner (or angle) of the block and the person's hips are impacting first. (A great way to dislocate or break your hips, this move.) Since there is no curve to bleed the energy off, a second impact will result as the block falls over again. *Ker-thud!* Great, so instead of getting clobbered once, you get nailed twice. Not good.

The trick about going over backward is to use your leg as a combination shock absorber and pole vault. Look at the photos below and on the following page.

What I'm doing here is using my foot/leg as a bridge (or pole vault) to fill the gap between my hips and the top of

*Backward roll.*

the pedestal. By placing my foot there, I not only begin to break my fall (not necessarily stop it, but slow it down), I begin to curl so my hips and spine form the now familiar curve. At this point, the leg begins to piston and create an extension of the curve so my hips don't hit square on. From there I gotta cop to getting fancy; nonetheless, I'm using the energy of the roll to spring back up. Curling into a tight ball takes you to where your feet are under you again and you can simply stand up. A diagram of what you're seeing is this:

18

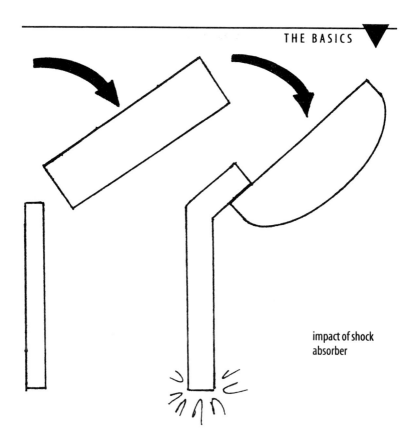

impact of shock
absorber

curving process begins

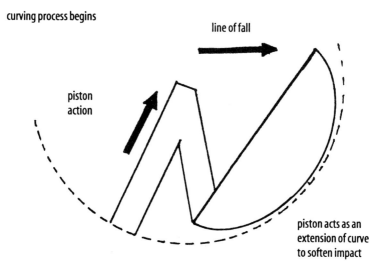

line of fall

piston
action

piston acts as an
extension of curve
to soften impact

19

That back leg is literally saving my ass by being a brake, shock absorber, piston, pole vault, and bridge. This is the up and down line of a roll that I mentioned earlier. Now this same principle works on a forward roll, but instead of your legs, you use your arms as the pistons and bridge.

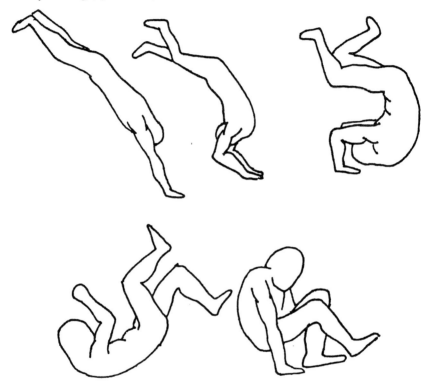

Actually, after looking at it, I just realized I should mention something else now instead of later like I planned. In both cases, I was using my arms and legs as pistons in both the beginning and later parts of the roll. Not only did the piston action absorb the energy on the way into the roll (shock absorber), but it pumped back out in the later part of the roll to get me back into a standing position.

Also, in a normal roll I would use the weight of my legs to pull me over. Near the end of the roll I'd put my legs out not only to give me something to land on but to shift weight forward so my body would be pulled in the direction I wanted to go. This weight shift is done near the end of the roll to add extra energy to the movement to give it the added force to complete itself. Legs are heavy, and by moving them around, their weight can be applied to getting you out of a roll faster.

In either a forward or backward roll, you protect your head by tucking it into your chest. You don't really want to take the impact or hold the weight of your body on your head or neck. If you reach back to where your neck meets your shoulders, you'll feel a bump on your spine. That's your seventh cervical vertebrae, called C-7 for short. It is where your neck stops and your back begins. From here on the vertebrae are bigger and stronger, and they are connected to other bones for structural support. A rule of thumb is that this is the farthest up you want to start your roll (or end it). The piston action of your arms is to allow you to protect your neck long enough to twist and begin to roll from here. You're less likely to snap your neck if you work from this point.

So a critical thing to remember about tumbling is that *your limbs are pistons!* Unless you've forgotten to put oil in your engine, pistons move. When pistons don't move, it means something is broken. If you try to meet a force of falling with stiff, unmoving arms, what gets broken are your arms. I knew of a kid who fell off the back of a truck. As he went over backward, he put both hands down to catch himself. It resulted in him having two broken arms and being in an upper body cast for six weeks. His arms were stuck out like some kind of scarecrow. He couldn't even feed himself or, worse, go to the john alone.

The trick of it is to balance enough force to slow you down or speed you up without locking yourself up. You lock in a tumble and you'll break something. Correctly applied, it can take only 7 or so pounds of pressure to break a bone. While our body is a marvel of engineering designed to absorb major impacts and not snap, there's only so much it can take before it throws in the towel.

What this action does is define the difference between martial arts falling and gymnastic falling. In gymnastics, you add energy into the process at key times to end up standing again. If you just rely on the roll and the energy of your falling, you won't make it back up. Remember, because of gravity, a dropped ball won't bounce up to the same level as you dropped it from. The same thing applies to you shining the floor with your butt. You have to add in extra energy to get back up.

## SHOULDER ROLLS

Now the next-door cousin to the up-and-down direction is diagonal. It is here that we encounter what is called a shoulder roll. Shoulder rolls are actually easier than forward and backward rolls. While you can use your arms as pistons and to extend the curve, your shoulder is a major part of the process. The same action you use to stick out and cave in your chest also rounds your shoulders for you. By trying to tuck your shoulder into your chest, you automatically curve your back. This roll is good for those odd-angle falls.

Again, the arms act as pistons, but instead of going in and out (to and from your body), they cross your body. This works both diagonally and horizontally, as needed by the situation. You can turn your arm in a variety of ways to make it a curve that leads into a shoulder roll. The energy of the fall is first absorbed in the process of folding your arm across your chest. That should slow you down enough for you to position your shoulder to continue the roll.

An important safety tip here is that you don't want to take an impact on an angle that jams your arm into your socket. Rather, you want to use your arm more like a turnstile. A turnstile spins the energy off while still allowing you to pass by. For example, if you have to take an impact, take it on the triceps side of your upper arm rather than on

22

*Shoulder roll.*

the forearm side of your elbow. With the former you can still bleed off enough energy to minimize damage while with the latter you can either dislocate your shoulder or break your arm.

23

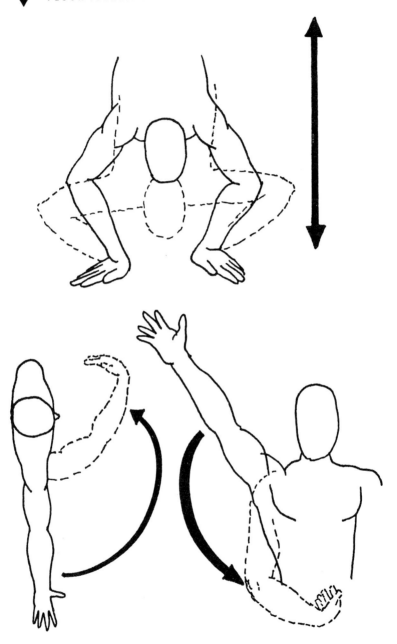

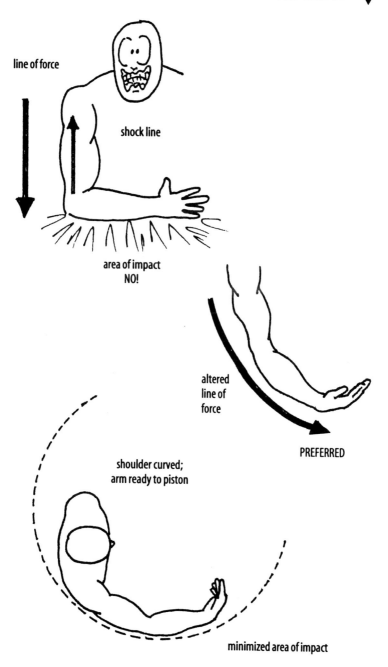

line of force

shock line

area of impact
NO!

altered
line of
force

PREFERRED

shoulder curved;
arm ready to piston

minimized area of impact

25

The thing to know about shoulder rolls is that often what will begin as a forward or back roll will end up as a shoulder roll. The physics of a falling body is an odd thing; it mostly depends on how you ended up falling in the first place, followed closely by your physical shape and design. Another factor in what could lead you to change your mind from doing a back roll to doing a shoulder roll is when you remember there's a table or something behind you. Suddenly, unless you want to kiss the furniture, you have to alter course in mid-tumble.

Most throws are designed to chuck you in this manner. While they initially curve around the guy during the throw, most people blow it when they straighten out during the landing. This is like snapping a wet towel down over your shoulder—though it's curved in flight, it whips out straight when it hits the ground. It's this straightening out that hurts you. By staying curled up around him or rolling when you land, you lessen the impact.

## SIDE ROLLS

The third angle of a curve is horizontal. Oddly enough, this applies to when you're about to fall on your face. The trick here is "twisting." Instead of nosediving it into the ground, you twist so you land on your shoulder or back, where the curve can take over.

The trick here is to take the energy of a forward fall and convert it into a rolling action to the side. The process involved is a combination of the piston action of the arms and their acting as a deflector as well. Your arms begin to deflect the energy from a straight fall to an angled one.

What this does is allows you to shed the energy of your fall into a different angle, which acts as propulsion that gets you out of range of your attacker. If the guy is expecting you to fall at his feet, he might be smart enough to have wound up for a kick to your precious face. By hitting the ground at a different angle and being in a roll when you first make contact, you can save yourself a boot in the face.

Wrong: bug on the windshield

Right: so cool he might not even lose his shades

## "THE POINT OF NO RETURN"

Probably the hardest part about any kind of roll is knowing when to abandon your feet to it. While your legs can be used to help break the fall, many people try to stay on their feet too long. What happens here is that their feet and legs get in the way of their roll. I myself have slammed my own knees into my

27

own knees into my face by trying to hang on too long. I've seen other people break their legs trying to hang on too long. Instead of the leg acting as a moving piston, the person ends up actually falling onto his leg. What often happens is that the person is still trying to exert enough force to overcome gravity, and this stiffens the leg. When his body weight lands on top of it, because he is tensed up and not rolling

*Horizontal fall.*

with the force, the leg (or even arm) has no choice but to break.

In a fall, there comes a point where you feel that you're going over. At this point, there is no question that you're going to hit the ground. We're going to call this "the point of no return." While you may have been trying to resist or slow the process of going over with your legs, when you hit this point, it's now time to get them out of the way.

By practicing balancing and tumbling, you can begin to sense where the point of no return is. This is the point beyond which there is no recovering. Start out by playing around to find out where your tip-over point is—where you simply keel over but by quickly putting your foot forward you can recover. The next step is to find that area from which you can't recover in time. A paranoid cat can land on its feet when dropped from something like 3 inches. You're not a cat, but it is possible to learn where your point of no return is.

Once you know what this point feels like, whenever you cross it, you'll know to immediately forget trying to recover your feet and start preparing to roll. This means 1) getting your feet out of the way so you don't fall on them, and 2) getting them away from any resistance and/or grounding that would interfere with your roll. The intent of the first is obvious. The latter means either getting your feet off the ground so as not to add resistance to your twist or out and away from any obstacle that they might hang up on. This can cause you to sprain or break your ankle. If you tripped over something, this is incredibly important. I've seen people in this situation get their foot broken on as little as quarter-inch snags.

The grounding part sounds sort of nebulous until you realize something. The top of your body can only twist so far before the bottom has to follow. If your lower portion is sitting there acting as dead weight, one of two things is going to happen: 1) your upper body twist will drag it along (unfortunately, the dead weight will slow down the process and make it less likely that your upper body will be able to carry the twist far enough to save you from impact), or 2) the weight of the lower portion will totally absorb the energy of the upper torso twist, causing the whole process to stall, and you'll hit the ground like a ton of lead.

The obvious answer to this problem is that when the warning bells go off that you've hit the point of no return (or heading toward it at too great a speed to possibly recover), your legs get into the act, too. Instead of sitting around waiting to be rescued, they kick off and out to help the process of the twist. This not only gets them out of the way so you don't land on them and break them, but it adds to the energy of the fall that you can later use to regain your feet.

Recommending that you speed up the process of hitting the ground may sound weird, but believe me, there is method to my madness. A few books back I mentioned that a trap usually is designed for you to attempt to fight it by pulling back. Sharks teeth, for example, are designed so if you try to pull back, you'll rip the shit out of yourself. However, the two best ways to handle traps are either not to get caught in the first place or to be too fucking tough for the trap.

My favorite example of this happened in Vietnam. This guy, who was fresh over from the World, was out with a patrol. Another patrol had gotten torn up a few days earlier and everyone was mightily pissed about it. As they walked along, this woman popped up out of nowhere and smiled at them. This was a restricted area where nobody was supposed to be, and they were on a dead-end trail. Everyone just watched her go by; when she was out of sight, they locked it down. The new guy was freaking out, saying, "This is a horseshoe, man! They told us in basic that it's ambush city!" One of the other guys slammed a grenade into his M79 and told the guy to shut the fuck up. When the ambush hit, it was the ambushers who got a rude surprise; their would-be victims were ready for them. It was a slaughter; none of the ambushers got away. Neither did the woman who signaled.

The same applies to getting knocked off your feet or thrown. The person who has compromised your balance is expecting you to go down where and how he wants you. By kicking in your own booster, you can break free of his control, and you don't want to go down under the control of another person. (I'm going to go into breaking holds in another chapter.) Suddenly the situation isn't what he expected. By taking control of your fall, you've left him holding nothing.

In the same sense (something we're going to explore later), if you can take your thrower down with you, his advantage disappears the moment he hits the ground with you. Suddenly, Captain Aikido has a choice: either he can follow you down to the ground or he can kiss his ear goodbye, because as you were passing by you grabbed onto it. Either he lets go and returns control of your flight to you, he follows and crashes with you, or he starts buying only one earring from now on.

In any case, what you do is break the control of the person doing the throwing, tripping, shoving, or knocking over. If it turns into a free-flight situation, when you land you've got the juice to pop back up. One of the best free-form sparring matches I ever got into was with a woman who had a traditionally earned black belt in aikido. In joking around, I reached out to bear swat her. She slipped and bounced me off a table. Her form was perfect, but with a little help from Ricochet Rabbit kung fu, I not only broke her grip but added an extra bounce and came flying back over the table at her. This was a Chinese woman, so when I say her eyes went round in shock as I tackled her, you get the idea of how surprised she was that her perfectly executed move had not worked. The match ended as a draw, with us lying on the floor in hysterics amid a wrecked house.

## THE "MUTT" FALL

The vertical twist is a very important technique to have under your belt, as it will help you with going over alone. It also is critical for making sure that you come out on top if you end up going over with someone else. What is important to realize is the twist is based in the mythical centerline that I have explained elsewhere.[2] You spin around that centerline that runs from the top of your head, through your body, out between your legs, and into the ground. When you're in the air, you simply twist around it. At that point it doesn't matter that you've lost your grounding. Even if the guy tackles you, he's going to be pushing harder on one side or the other so you roll with the force. In the process of rolling, you can often use the same energy to break free of his grip.

Another type of fall is a total mutt of the other three. This is going over sideways. Everything I've mentioned thus far comes into play in this roll. It's officially an up/down roll, but it combines a cross-step piston action with the arm piston action of a diagonal roll and the body motion of a vertical twist.

The most difficult part of this roll is using your leg as a cross piston. Unless you're well-versed in Chinese or South Pacific fighting arts, most people don't work well with crossed feet, rolling ankles, and folding knees. It's here that stunt work or a gymnastics instructor really helps. The object is to fold one leg in while simultaneously cross-stepping with your other leg to act as a piston to slow your fall. This allows you to slow down enough to begin the horizontal twist and roll out of the way. Often this means that you'll end up rolling backward, as I did in the photo.

• • • • • • •

Any of these situations can happen at any time in normal life, which makes this important to know anyway, but during a fight you really have to know how to minimize the damage from a fall. The thing you have to remember is that fights seldom happen in wide open, softly padded places. There are usually things like furniture, walls, other people, and equipment which you'll be either slamming into or rolling over.

Once, in a hurry to get into the back of a retreating truck, I did an odd rolling high jump/tumble into the bed. I was not particularly amused by the fact that, in the process of landing, I rolled over an upturned shovel. If I had landed square on that shovel rather than rolling over it, I would have been seriously hurt. The process of rolling over something actually minimizes the amount of damage that you receive, whereas landing squarely on top of it like a block increases the damage. You have to know that you might slam into things or roll over bystanders in the process of saving your ass.

Knowing this, however, you can begin to practice these rolls to minimize the damage. If you can't get to a gym or school, find a grassy place and start practicing slow and tight at first. I'm talking about starting on your knees and rolling forward, backward, diagonally, and to the sides. As you learn to keep everything curved (and believe me, you'll know when it isn't curved enough), begin to work your way up in height.

Remember, immediately springing back up is just as important as minimizing the damage of the fall. Gentleman Jim is a myth in a real fight. Comparatively speaking, I'm a nice guy, but I'll still kick a man who's down in a hot New York second. Shit, if he's down, I'm going to make sure he stays there.

# FOOTNOTES

[1] In fact, if you're a parent or intend to live long enough to become one, I highly recommend you send your children to a gymnastics class. Because of this ability, I survived most childhood accidents with minimum damage, including a head-on collision with a car on my bicycle, from which I walked away with only a scar on my wrist. If nothing else, it will keep your medical bills down.

[2] See my video, *Surviving a Street Knife Fight: Realistic Defensive Techniques*, available from Paladin Press.

# ▼2 BREAKING GRIPS

*"Animal, you could fuck up a wet dream!"*
—Tim Toohey

It may not come as a surprise to you, but I was the sort of kid who always was taking apart my toys. I wanted to see how they worked. On top of that, you'd never know where I'd pop up or what was going to happen because I was always looking at things from different angles. Needless to say, I was always finding out unique ways to hot-wire a situation.[1]

It was from these experiences that I began to realize that any system or process can be screwed up. Even the best has weaknesses and holes where a well-applied monkey wrench can bring the whole thing either crashing down or to a screaming halt. The same could be said about traps—even the best have weaknesses or ways out that can foil them.

This attitude led me to look at martial arts techniques in a different light. I was less concerned about perfecting certain moves than I was in knowing how to fuck 'em up when someone tried them on me. Just as a candy bar down the gas tank of a car can render it pretty useless, I wanted to know the weak points in any move.

I must admit, I became keenly interested in counters to techniques during a particular fight where I did a spinning heel kick as the guy countered with a front snap kick. It was bad enough that the guy had made me look like a chipmunk with my nuts in my cheeks, but he then had the temerity to try and kick them back into their original position. As my friends dragged him off me, I swallowed hard to put everything back and decided I had better start looking at fighting in a different light.

I have to tell you, I'm not down on judo or aikido. If I have a problem with anything, it is the same old routine that I've grumbled about before: *don't try to pass it off as something it isn't.* There are four categories that a so-called martial art can fall into: 1) self-defense, 2) a physical discipline or art form, 3) a spiritual discipline, or 4) a tournament/sport. It's a rare person, and we're talking hen's teeth here, who can encompass all four aspects and teach them all. What bugs me is when someone masters one aspect and then tries to peddle it as all of them. I admit I get my nose out of joint when I see some wanker teaching numbers two or four and telling innocent people that it's self-defense. It's not applied self-defense; it's either an art/discipline or it's a sport. Calling it something else is misleading. It's the student who's going to try something in a real self-defense situation that any 14-year-old street kid knows how to counter. It's not the teacher who goes to the hospital or gets robbed; it's the poor schmuck who believed his garbage and got blindsided for trusting him.

Putting it bluntly, the moves are different. In an actual self-defense situation, you're dealing with a mugger/rapist who has an entirely different set of priorities than standing around and exchanging blows in a sparring match. His purpose has nothing to do with fighting. In fact, it's not going to be a "fight"; it's going to be an assault. He wants to hurt you, and he wants to do it before you can hurt him. Most streetfights involve two guys snarling until one suddenly moves. Usually, the guy who moves first is the winner. This is because the advantage is immediately gained and then exploited. No back and forth sparring here, folks. One guy gains the advantage and keeps whaling on his victim until the guy is down. Once there, if the attacker isn't finished yet, the sucker on the floor is going to get seriously stomped.

Fighters who are trained in actual combat systems or have mucho experience know a very important thing which escapes most American-trained martial artists as well as the bulk of the general population: putting a guy on the ground usually wipes out his effectiveness. While I may grouse at formalized technique that has little actual application, I must point out that judo, aikido, and ju-jutsu are, if not based entirely on it, aware of this fact, while kali and silat are two combat systems gruesomely effective at achieving this end.

As a bouncer and event security, I learned that the best way to end a situation quickly and avoid lawsuits was to knock the guy down.[2] As a streetfighter, I discovered early on that the faster I got most people down, the safer I was. It's hard to draw a weapon when you're not only lying on it but your eyes are crossed from slamming into the ground.

I always say that there is no such thing as a guarantee in a fight. Well the closest that you'll ever encounter to a guarantee is that an experienced fighter will try to get you onto the ground. He's going to do this by 1) hitting you hard enough that you fall down, 2) tripping you, or 3) throwing you. Most people don't really watch their feet (or footwork) in a fight and are therefore extremely vulnerable to attacks that will blow their feet out from under them. Heel hooks, body checks, tripping, stepping on feet, and sweeps are things that, if I went into here, would make this book an encyclopedia. A more experienced or combat-system-trained fighter will use these as his primary way to get you down to the ground. You must put serious distance between yourself and these people. If you fall in their attack range, you're dog meat. With these guys, all four laws of ground fighting apply in spades.

Fortunately, these guys are relatively rare. What you're most likely to encounter is someone who grabs you and drags you over. This can be done in some basic or some fancier ways. The basic ways rely on raw muscle, while the fancier rely on proper grip, speed, motion, and gravity. It may come as a surprise to you, but the basic ways are harder to counter. While the fancier methods can be blindingly fast, they are easier to escape from if you know the warning signs and can react in time. The problem is, if you don't get away from them, they can also cause more damage. A gorilla might physically grab you and muscle you down to the ground, but someone who knows how to do the fancy-dan stuff will blast you into a wall at a hundred miles an hour.

In this chapter, we're going to be dealing with the common grabs/holds and how to break free from them before a face-to-face meeting with Mr. Wall or Mr. Table. One thing that my old teacher Oberon drilled into me was how to break holds. Believe me, when that monster grabbed on to you, all you wanted to do was get away. Seventeen-inch arms and growing up in East L.A. made him someone you didn't want to have muckle on to you. Nothing like having someone try to wad you up like a used Kleenex to convince you that it was time to break away.

If you can't break away from a grip, the person who is throwing you is still in control of your flight path. As long as that person is glommed on to you, he is going to be restricting your motion. This leads to: 1) you're going to where he wants you to go. If this is face first into a wall, you've got a problem. 2) You can twist only so far before something snaps. His breaking your arm usually ends a fight in his favor. 3) He can control not only where but how hard you're going to land. Believe me, he's not going to be on your side when it comes to this. 4) You're only able to defend yourself with the part that isn't being restricted. While he may not be able to hit you with his right hand because it's holding you, his friend has no such restrictions.

The secret of breaking a grip is in the construction of the hand. Few proper martial arts grips are the simple grab that you're likely to encounter by an eager but untrained anthropoid. Nonetheless, we're going to start there, since it's what you're going to encounter the most.

## BREAKING THE GORILLA GRIP

I don't know that there is a proper name for this grip, and even if there is, it's probably in a foreign language, so I'm just going to call it the "gorilla grip."

The history of the gorilla grip is one steeped in tradition and mysticism. First discovered by a Neanderthal martial arts master named "Oook,"[3] it has been passed down through countless generations and is still in wide use today by many of Oook's distant (and, in some cases, not so distant) descendants. It works on lower limbs, clothing, hair, ears, and, in some cases, upper arms and shoulders. It is the preferred grip of those with opposable thumbs.

There are several things that you can do when it comes to dealing with this grip. The major deciding factor is, how big and/or strong are the guy's hands? If the guy has got monstrous flippers, you may have a serious problem when he wraps one around your wrist or your hair. Another determining factor is the strength of his hands. I'm a small guy with small hands, but I got a grip like a crocodile. That often equalizes the disadvantage of small hands. Someone who uses his hands in his work (like picking up bricks) is going to be a drag to try and break free from.

The easiest way out of the gorilla grip is through the junction where the thumb lies across the fingers. Look at the illustration on page 41 and see where the energy can be applied for escape.

The thing to know about this grip is that the more closed it is, the harder it is to escape from. A person who grabs you by the shirt in this grip will literally be making a fist with your shirt clamped inside, while someone grabbing you by the arm will have his hand around a tube that his

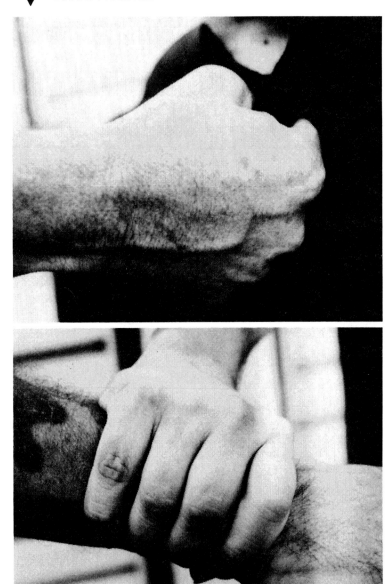

*Gorilla grips.*

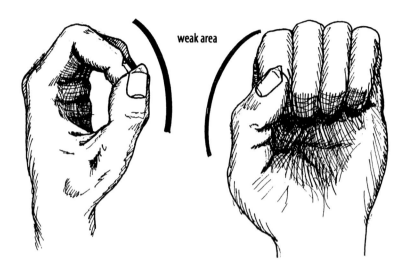

weak area

fingers may or may not reach all the way around. The latter is easiest to escape from. This is why the size of someone's hands has so much to do with how you escape from this grip. I've been grabbed by people who could almost scratch their third knuckle with their thumb while holding my wrist. No way was I going to twist my way out of that one. In cases like that, it calls for plan B. Plan B is to apply pressure to his hand via your body weight and get the hell out of Dodge. We'll go into that in a bit.

The real trick to accomplishing the most common escape lies in one of two actions: twisting or levering. Unless you're shaped really odd, your forearm near your wrist is wider than it is deep. You have to turn this width to your advantage. In your forearm, you have two bones lying side by side. The outside one that makes up your elbow is the ulna; the one near your thumb is the radius. Positioning these in the weak point of his hand is the key to escaping a grip.

By twisting your wrist/forearm in such a manner that one of these two bones rests against the thumb/finger junction of your holder, you've positioned yourself for an escape. If the person has a good hold on you, you'll

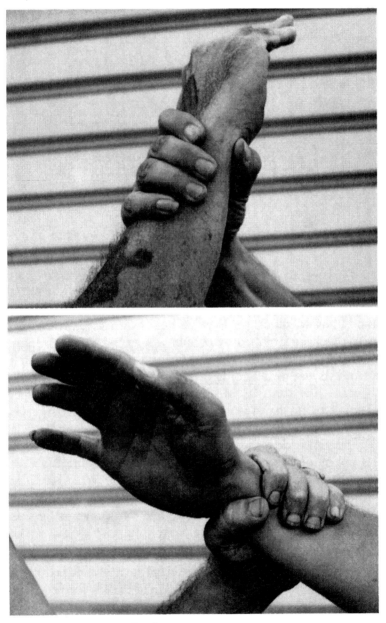

*Positioning your wrist for an escape.*

probably give yourself an Indian burn from the friction, but better that than needing dental work.

Getting yourself into this position also does another very important thing—it positions you in a manner where your arm is the strongest. From here, your biceps muscle can be used for a sudden inward jerk to break free, or your triceps and shoulder for a downward or outward jerk. By pulling away in a direction that your arm is naturally strong, you increase your chances for escape.

At this point, you quickly jerk your hand out from the person's grip. Back toward you or out from him works best, as the secret of this move is to put pressure on the thumb/finger junction. Going out or back prevents him from moving his arm in such a way to compensate for the pressure you're putting on his grip. By moving outward, you move to the extent of his reach.

Although bending inward allows you to move in the direction your arm is strongest, if he can move his arm in the same direction as you're going, he can counter your move. By following, the pressure on his grip will be reduced. That means he might be able to hang on. If, on the other hand (no pun intended), you can maneuver your hand to the extent of his reach before (or as) you jerk away, all of the pressure is going to hit the weak junction of his thumb/fingers. Unless the guy is King Kong, your arm is going to be stronger than his hand.

The next way out of the gorilla grip is via "levering." The trick is to lever your arm off the person's palm, not (as many people try to do) where his fingers and thumb are locked onto you. If you try to do that, you end up driving your arm deeper into his grip. You can wiggle all day long trying to lever out of a grip in the wrong direction. Since the person can move his arm, he can compensate for the pressure you'd be applying against his grip's lock. By following you, he can keep you from ever reaching the point where the misapplied lever would reach the breaking point of his grip.

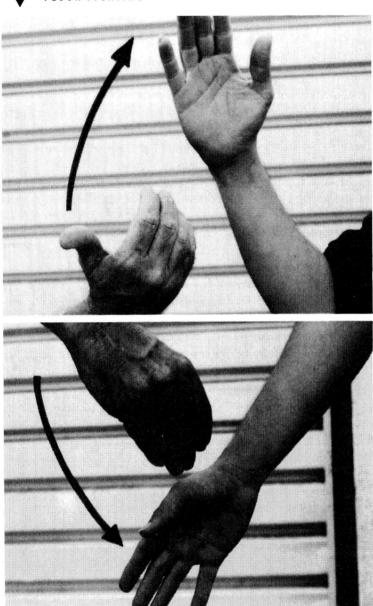

*Breaking a grip.*

A properly directed lever uses his own hand against him. Either his own muscle tension is going to give you the leverage you need to break free, or he's going to reach a point where his wrist won't turn anymore. Once this point is hit, either you go free or he gets a broken wrist. Do it fast enough and it could be yes on both counts.

When it comes to levering, your key concern again is his thumb/finger junction. That's where you need to break free from. Now you can either twist as mentioned earlier to

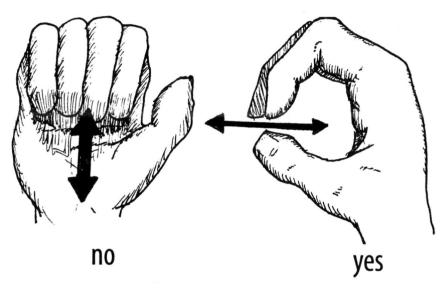

## no                                          yes

make it more effective, or you can lever straight out of a grip. While the latter is possible, that added twist does help the process.

The fastest lever action is to use the little finger side of his palm as a pivot point. This is especially effective if he's got a serious grip on you, as his muscle tension to hold you also stiffens his hand, so you can use it as a springboard. Perhaps the easiest way to describe the action is, using his pinky side as a pivot point, you roll your arm around to the back of his hand. Look at the illustration and you'll see what I mean.

Now, even if the guy tries to roll with your levering action, there's going to come a point where his wrist can't turn any-more. When that happens, the pressure is applied to the junc-tion and you pop free. The trick here is to remem-ber to move in small circles from your elbow.

A more diffi-cult way of doing it is by using the thumb side of his hand as your pivot point. Instead of trying to roll around to the back of his hand from the pinky side, you roll around from his thumb side. The angle is slightly different since you must lever out diagonally down toward his wrist to escape his fingers.

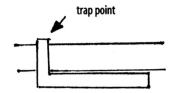

trap point

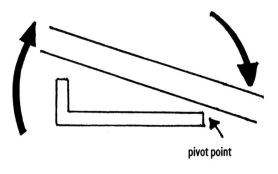

pivot point

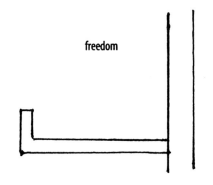

freedom

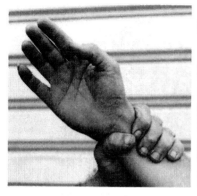

*Levering.*

The reason this is harder to do is because the direction that you're going is usually toward your grabber. By heading into his space, it's easier for him to roll his arm inward and compensate for the pressure you're trying to apply to the junction. To do this, you have to be awfully quick, and he has to seriously be trying to muscle you. This is one of those situations that occasionally pop up if the guy grabs you weird or if you're struggling. It's less likely to work in a face-to-face grapple than the first one, but if the chance arises, take it. Where this one really seems to work is when someone grabs you from your side in a cross-handed grab.

These escapes work well against someone who either isn't fast enough to compensate or strong enough to counter your moves. I have to tell you that certain moves work better from particular angles. If you've been grabbed face to face by someone and your hands are up near your face, a lever action using the thumb side as a pivot point is just flat-out not going to work. You'd have to reach way over

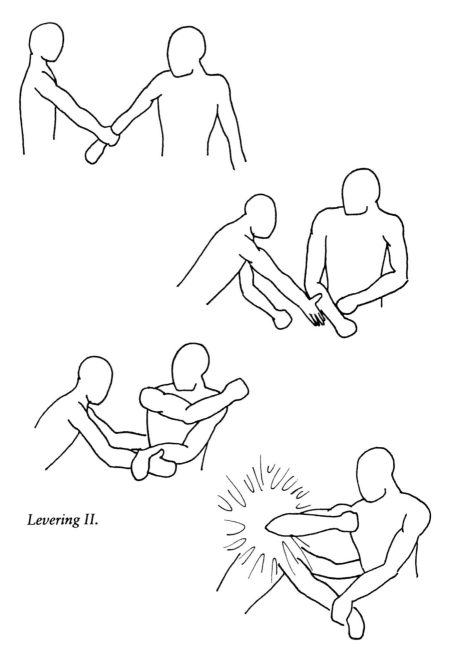

*Levering II.*

your opponent's head and have an extra joint in your arm in order to be able to reach a point where the necessary pressure would be applied to the grip's junction. Unless you're grappling with a midget, you're not going to be tall enough to do it.

What you have to do is literally grab a friend and practice these things. Your body has to know the necessary angle to escape from any position. I've given you the basic physics that you'll need to figure out the angle you can use to escape. Where this begins to become critical is when someone is in the process of tossing you. The hardest thing to do is to be able to do two things at once instinctively. One is knowing how to tumble and land to minimize the damage. The other is to break free of the person's grip in mid-flight. If you don't, he's going to be interfering with your ability to land safely. As long as he is controlling your flight, you're going to get hurt. Instinctively breaking free of a grip, even if you're going down, will minimize your chances of getting hurt.

## PUNCHING OUT OF A GRIP

Every now and then you're going to encounter a nightmare. This is the guy who's got a set of paws that rightly belong on a giant, who's got a grip like a vise, or who's got the experience to never allow you to turn or wiggle to a point where you can lever or twist out of the weak junction of his hand. These people do exist out there, and they are a pain in the ass to deal with. It is here that you begin to use that pivot/centerline that I've mentioned before. This line is inside you, and you spin around it. While many of these techniques can be done without it, most of them work much better if you use the pivot point as the source of the moves. Since the horizontal roll I showed you earlier is based in this same action, it shouldn't be too much of a problem to incorporate.

Your best way to deal with this situation is to punch or draw. The physics are basically the same, as the action goes in line with the person's grip on your arm and allows you to blow through the trapping point.

The punch is exactly that. The guy has got ahold of you and you fire a punch down the same line as his grip. The most effective form is a tight uppercut or a real boxing hook. Both of these use your entire body weight. This is why the pivot comes into play—by using it you incorporate your body weight. The purpose of this action is not to try to break free of the person's grip using your arm muscles alone, but to break free using the force of your entire body in motion. There are very few people who can keep a grip on someone's body weight in motion. It's also instinctive for

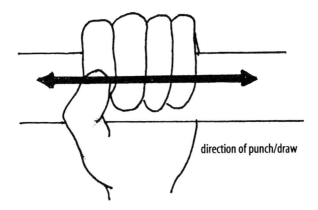

direction of punch/draw

him to try to clamp down and hold you to keep from getting punched. This locks his arm and puts all the force into his hand. On a silver platter man, on a silver platter. Also, if you punch correctly, you're going to twist your arm and spread his grip in the process, which aids and abets your escape.

Even if you don't immediately break free of the grip, you'll shift the location of his grip further up your arm. In the larger area of your arm, his grip is enlarged and the junction between thumb and fingers is weaker. This means that you can use the twist and levering techniques you just learned. The real cookie about this is not only do you get a chance to break free, but if your punch lands you compound the guy's problems. He not only has to try to keep ahold of you, he must also deal with the shock of getting popped one from an unexpected side.

Now one of the things that judo and aikido rely on is the committed punch of karate and amateur fighters. A double boxing jab kind of blows most of their techniques out of the water. If you fire a shot at someone and he slips and tries to grab you, a second jab with that hand usually will blow his grip. Of course, a left/right jab combo against a known throwing stylist is also a definite giggle. Throw the first punch wide enough so he slips inside and have the other one waiting for him.

Probably the most effective utilization of your body weight is when the guy grabs you by your clothing in a gorilla grip. In case you didn't know, a thunderin' herd of judo throws are based in grabbing clothes this way. When someone grabs you like this, the nastiest response you can give him is a straight shot to the chest. You aim for his centerline with a Nighty Nite Bunny Rabbit. I know elsewhere I've maintained that punches to the chest are a waste of time, but these are special circumstances. If you can snake in an uppercut to the diaphragm, it's a total beauty. If you can't, then try to drive his sternum out past his shoulder blades.

The purpose of this shot is twofold. One, purely and simply, is to impact his system. If you can rack his diaphragm up, not only is the force going to lift him but he's going to be more concerned about breathing than tossing you. The main point of this part, however, is to mess up his motion. He's traveling in a direction that is going to result in you on your head if he gets there. A force coming in at 90 degrees is not only going to alter his course, but if you hit hard enough, it might blow him off his feet. Remember, his stance integrity is going one way so he can throw you; a 90-degree impact could send him over backwards.

The second fold of the twofold reason has to do with

losing his grip. While it is possible to grab someone so your knuckles are against his chest (the "bomber" grip [4]), you often have to settle for something less. More often, the cloth is clutched in such a way that the palms and pad of the thumb are against the chest, and the same physics of the weak junction apply. This lesser grip is susceptible to impact, which is where the NNBR into the chest comes into play.

Of course, a "sneaker punch" (as described by Jack Dempsey in his book *Championship Fighting*) works like a dream. The object of this punch is to hit the person so hard that his arms extend fully out. Not only does it interrupt his travel plans and make it harder to throw you with extended arms, but from here there is a chance that he'll lose his grip on your clothes. If he doesn't have a solid grip, he will lose hold. If that happens, the likelihood of him being able to do the move effectively are seriously reduced. Even if he doesn't lose his grip, there's a good chance he'll go over backwards. If he takes you with him, what we are going to cover in the next chapter will make him regret not letting go of you in the first place.

These two things combine into a nasty combination that screws up the effectiveness of these moves. Even if he manages to throw you, that peg to the chest is going to slow him down long enough for you to do something else to prevent your getting damaged. Another cute move is, as he spins his body weight one way, you pivot yours the other way. For example, if he tries to peel off to your left, you peel off to your right. This puts your body weight in contest with his. The only thing that is keeping them together is his grip. Your body weight going one way, his going the other, and his hand trying to hold them together—yeah right. If you further state your case by including an overhand hook to his head from the side that is closest to him, you might really be able to convince him to reconsider.

A punch is effective for a variety of reasons, not the least of which is if the guy is throwing you and you ring his chimes as you're going down, it'll probably catch him off guard. He's going to have to recover from the punch before he can press his advantage. As he's doing that, you're recovering your feet. I've surprised a few folks by unexpectedly pegging them one upside the head as I was heading for the floor. Since I was twisting to land anyway, it was no big deal to add in a punch as I was passing by.

Probably the most effective part of this kind of pivot punching is you can shift the punch he's trying to use against you into a shoulder/body check by tightening in

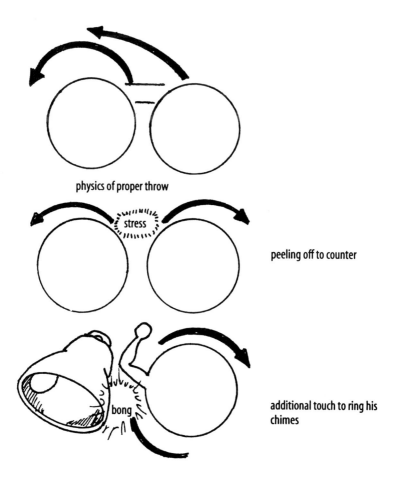

physics of proper throw

peeling off to counter

additional touch to ring his chimes

your original circle (the spin around your pivot/centerline). A similar counter is suddenly reversing your body's spin. While he's messing with your one hand, the cavalry is coming in from the other direction. Since most throws rely on the person slipping your punch into either the inside or outside gate, he is vulnerable to a shift in directions. Suddenly you are slamming him at a 90-degree angle to his stance integrity. He has a choice: abandon the throw or get knocked on his ass. I gotta tell you, though, this is a seriously advanced technique. Not that it is physically difficult to do; it's actually easy. What is hard is being aware

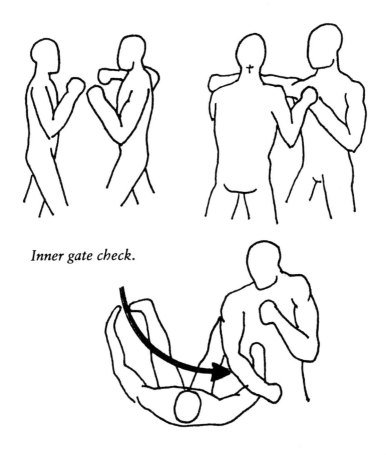

*Inner gate check.*

*Outer gate check.*

enough and fast enough to shift your direction that quickly. Oh yeah, and being in balance enough to change directions that quickly is sort of rough.

## DRAWING OUT OF A GRIP

While the photos show the best possible example of what I was talking about, you'd better be ready to hit the floor with the guy if you try this move. The odds are that he will grab you and try to take you down with him. That's okay, we'll get into landing on your opponent in a bit. In the meantime, what will counter his counter to your counter is a strategically placed draw.

The draw works along the same line as the punch, as it goes with the line of the grip. Unlike the punch, though, the draw is a retreating move. Of course, by its nature, as one hand retreats the other hand is in the perfect position to strike, but we won't mention that right now.

*Draw without check.*

The draw basically is a reversed punch along the pivot/centerline. Instead of spinning forward, you're spinning back. The elbow is kept tucked tight against the body so the body weight is utilized instead of the arm muscles.

While the punch can be a little off line with the guy's grip, the draw has to be on line. If you try to draw from a different angle, what usually happens is you end up dragging the guy into you. The draw, by itself, relies on getting to the extent of his arm and then overpowering his grip with your body weight. If you try to do it catiwompus to the guy's grip or in a place where you should lever/twist out, it's just going to drag him along. Since the action is toward you, the obvious result is he's going to slam into you. Boy, that was graceful.

One pointer on making the draw really effective is to twist your wrist/arm as you do it. If your palm is pointing down when you start the move, it should have rotated so it's pointing up when the move is finished. This added twisting action makes the draw a real bear to hang onto.

The pièce de résistance of the draw, however, is the "check/sweep" that you can do with it. As you're drawing back, your other hand is setting up a roadblock for anyone silly enough to follow. Your arm passes through, but anyone trying to come along for the ride gets clotheslined off. There are two ways of doing a check like this. One is where the other hand sweeps along the top of your arm, and the other is when it sweeps along the bottom. In either case, the side of your palm impacts into any uninvited guests and sweeps them off. The over/underhand is purely a matter of choice. While the underhand sweep positions you better for a few nasty-assed advance moves, they both work real well.

## DEALING WITH ADVANCED GRIPS

The final thing I wish to address here is the more advanced grips that the throwing systems use. Here's the problem. While they're technically easier to escape from,

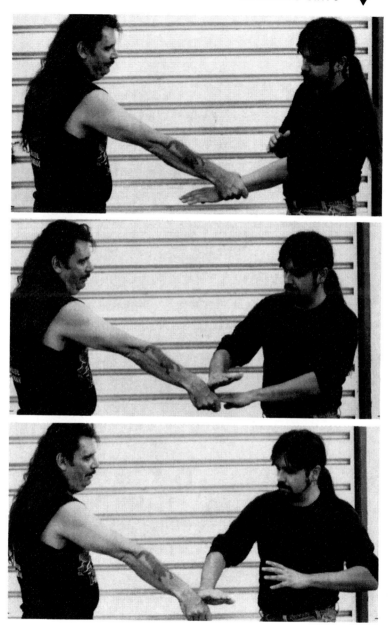

*Drawing with check I.*

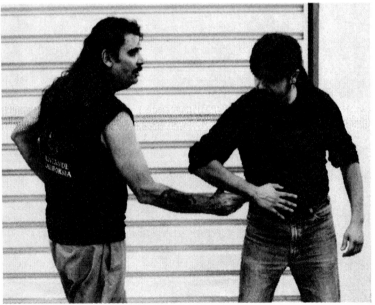

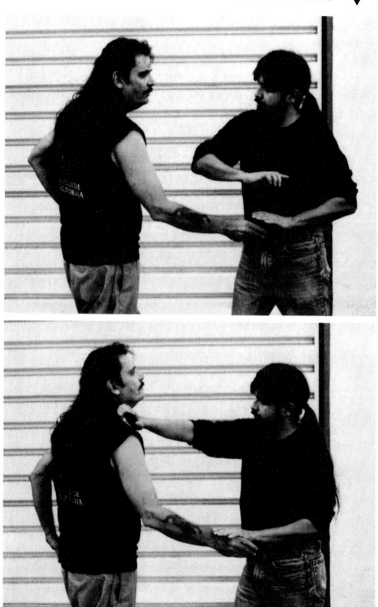

*Draw with check II.*

the people who use them are often lightning quick on getting you into them. The aikido move of *koda gieesh* leaves a major hole for you to slip out of. There is no connection between thumb and fingers.

Either the twist or the draw will get you out of this move with zippo fuss . . . if you have time. Most of these grips rely on you trying to resist them a certain way. This type of resistance is futile, because it's what they want you to do. While you're messing around resisting, they're up to something else. What they are not expecting is for you to go jackrabbiting off in another direction.

The best way to escape is to head in the same direction they want you to go, but too fast for them to control. *Koda gieesh* is effective because by the time most people think of heading toward the actual exit, the person using the grip has moved his victim's limb into a position where it can no longer turn that way. In simpler terms, he's twisted your arm to a point where you can't escape.

*Koda gieesh.*

Another common trick is to grab the thumb and lever it over. Stick your right hand out in front of you, palm down. Now turn your hand so your thumb turns down and points to the ground. I'm going to call this direction counterclockwise (cause it is). The thumb turning up is clockwise. What happens here is someone grabs your thumb and twists it in one of these ways. Eventually you either end up on your head or bent over with your arm sticking out behind you. This move has a proper name, which, as is my normal operating procedure, I've totally spaced out.

In the counterclockwise motion, you end up bending over and your arm sticking out behind you with a locked elbow. In the clockwise direction, if you go far enough you'll end up throwing yourself onto your own head to avoid a broken wrist. If the guy gets your left hand instead, you get the same action going the other direction, but for clarification purposes, I'm going to speak as if it's your right hand that is being grabbed.

This grip's greatest strength is controlling the thumb until it gets you to the danger zone. Until you know how to escape properly, everything you'd do while trying to save your thumb in this situation will actually put you closer to the danger zone. You may move to avoid getting your thumb snapped off, but what you are doing is putting yourself in a position where your elbow can be controlled. Remember, he who controls the elbow controls the fight.

In order to escape this move, you must either drag your thumb out of his grip in a sort of minidraw move or cock your elbow. We'll look at the dynamics of the draw first.

While you can try to draw toward yourself, you have to relax your thumb immediately for it to be effective. A relaxed thumb angles in the same direction of the pull, thereby making it harder for him to hold onto. If you try to keep your thumb stiff, it will give him something to hang onto. In this situation you may not be able to get free before you break your own thumb.

If you can't get out before he clamps down, you're still

going to have to draw out, but in a different direction. Often what will happen in this situation is the person will begin to twist your wrist either clockwise or counterclockwise. Unlike *koda gieesh*, you can't get out by Speed Racer'n it where he wants you to go. When he starts spinning you clockwise or counterclockwise, you need to pull your thumb out straight along the line of his grip. I'm talking up and down here. He is spinning you in a circle; you have to shoot straight out from that circle in order to escape.

Now don't think you're going to be able to shoot out in a perfectly straight line. His turning your wrist/arm is going

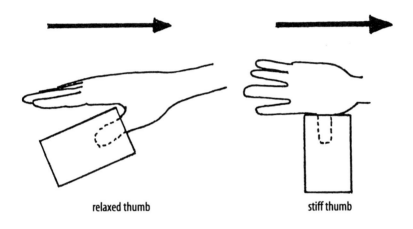

relaxed thumb                              stiff thumb

to make your actual move a weird crescent gesture. However it is easier to understand what the physics are if it's put in straight line example. Practice this move with a friend and you'll see what I mean by it being a weird course. Now don't have him try to crush your finger at first with a mondo gorilla grip. Not only is it unlikely that anyone will be able to slap that intense of a grip on you as fast as it takes to grab you, but what you do in the face of that intense of a grip is different.

The draw has to be done before he gets a full grip on

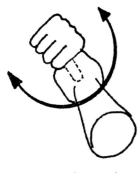

direction of spin

direction of draw

your thumb. Believe it or not, there is going to be a moment's lag between the time his hand first contacts your thumb and when he locks down into the grip. You have to train yourself to draw out of there instinctively when someone hits your hand or thumb with a slap. If he slaps and you start drawing immediately, the odds are against him being able to lock down on you.

If someone grabs onto your right thumb and twists in a counterclockwise motion, you will end up with your elbow facing up if you go far enough. If you allow this to happen to you, you haven't screwed the pooch, you have out and out fucked the dog. In short, you're dead, bottom line. The entire move was designed to get you into this exact position. Once you are there, the person drops a second hand onto the back of your elbow and has you locked in that same bent-over position that cops love to drop troublemakers into. Your arm is locked and levered against you, and it only takes a little pressure to plant you face-first into the concrete.

In the clockwise motion, what often will happen is the guy will end up committing a second hand to the process. See, his wrist will only go so far, so it actually poops out around the time that you'd be debating whether to launch to save your thumb. So what the second hand does is get your pinky side palm caught and continues the process where his other hands wrist crapped out.

Now then there, buckaroos, I'm gonna share with you one of the main weaknesses that nasty folks like me have found about them there throwing styles. As good as the throwing styles are, they often make the mistake of committing both hands to a process. Against an experienced fighter, this would be bad. Anytime two hands are in one place, they can end up imitating fishing line and get tangled up. Pivot/draw/check is the best way to make sure this happens.

Let's say that somebody has managed to slap you into one of these grips. You lock your upper arm against your body and begin to use your centerline/pivot to move your body weight. You're not resisting the action against your thumb since your elbow and wrist aren't locked against the pressure. What you're doing is adding your two cents. At this time, no joint has gotten to the lock-out point, so you can still get away with moving this way. By locking your upper arm against you, you begin to draw the whole operation toward you via the irresistible force of your moving body weight.

It is here that you put pebbles in front of homeboy's skateboard. Remember the check/sweep that I mentioned earlier? Now is the time to release the dogs of war. As you ·draw back, a check/sweep will not only blow his grip loose, but if he has both hands involved, it will bind his hands. For this particular move, the underarm sweep works best, as it is more likely to catch both hands by impacting on his wrists instead of striking his fingers as the overarm sweep does.

From that point, with both his hands bound and shoved to the side and one of your hands free, I'll let you figure out your next move. I'll give you a hint though—it has to do with hitting him so hard that even his momma will fall down.

What the next move has in common with the thumb grip is that it's main intention is to tie you up long enough for the person to get control of your elbow. Unlike a thumb grip, it consists of bending your wrist back to achieve the

*Sweep, check, and strike!*

lock. Also, unlike the thumb grip, it usually only results in the bent-over, arm-sticking-out-from-behind-you position. This is the famous police lock grip that they so often put bad boys into.

It's quick, it's easy, and it uses people's natural action against them. If I were to try to reach out and grab your hand, you would normally pull back. The common way of pulling back does most of the work for the person attempting this grip. In short, you move your arm exactly where he wants it. From there it's just a matter of stepping in and taking it a step further. This is not good.

The question now is, if your normal action is being used against you, how do you mess up the new dance? The answer works both with the thumb grip and this move. It's bend your elbow and, if necessary, pivot.

If he is trying to get you into a position where your elbow is locked straight behind you, does it not make sense that a bent elbow would foil his original goal? Since the original move consists of your arm swinging down in an arc, what you do is change the direction. We're going to use the clock method here. Your head is 12 o'clock; if you were to stick your arm straight out in front, it would be at 3 o'clock. What this move does is move your arm around to 9 o'clock and lock it out. With his second hand on your elbow, you cannot pivot your shoulder to spin your arm. Therefore it behooves you not to stay out later than 7 o'clock.

In fact, at 6 o'clock is when you're going to change the tune. What I'm going to show you has a weakness that a good fighter can still exploit. Fortunately there is a counter to his counter of your counter. (Welcome to advanced fighting. Like two snakes wrestling, it has layers and layers. This is what goes on between good fighters.) Fortunately, there aren't that many good fighters out there, so this basic move works most of the time.

The second that you realize that the guy is following your arm's movement by slipping to your side, you change course. Instead of continuing the move, you abort.

Generally, this will happen around 6 o'clock, which puts you in a perfect position to do what I'm going to tell you. Bend your elbow and jerk your arm up. The action is the same as if you were to suddenly decide to slam your elbow into the face of the person who is trying to slip you. (Hint hint, nudge nudge.[5])

If this does not break the grip that the person has on you immediately (and if the guy is fast, it might not), you have to throw a pivot in there immediately. If not, the guy can shift his direction and end up with you in a different, but equally nasty, predicament.

Instead of locking your elbow out behind you, the new move is to lock your wrist back and elevate your arm. What you end up in is a position very much like if you got your arm caught in the cookie jar. I was taught this move by an aikidoist bouncer who would use this move at the bar. He'd put his hand on the guy's wrist and wait for the guy to pull up and away. When that happened, the bouncer would lock the wrist and the elbow way up high. The guy ends up jumping onto his tippy toes to avoid the pain. He'd then escort the gentleman to the door. In case you haven't caught on by now, it's hard enough to throw an effective punch across your body. The further complication of standing like a ballerina makes it even harder to do. Once that wrist lock is achieved, you're screwed; there is no safe way out.

If the thumb/wrist grab happens to you and you counter the attempted lock out, nine times out of ten it will work. It's when the guy starts following your new position that you're in a heap of shit, because it means he's a pro. Basically, the only thing you can do is pivot that side forward immediately to prevent the lock-out from happening. This tears your arm out of his grasp and, hopefully, reach. Don't try to pivot back at him since he has his hands in a perfect situation to check that action. Just keep going and buy yourself distance.

Also, don't waste time trying to punch or kick. I don't care if you're Jack Dempsey, you can't knock someone out with a cross-body punch. That would be the only way to stop this move—a one-shot knockout punch. It ain't gonna happen. Trying either the cross body punch or an elbow shot would be suicide. Not only do they have a snowball's chance of working, but they take you right back into the neighborhood where the shit wasn't going your way in the first place. That means there's more time for something else to go wrong. You have to escape by dragging your arm out of that place.

Now the seriously bad news is that in order to escape in this manner, you're going to have to turn your back to the person. We're talking last-ditch movement here anyway. As you're twisting away, you are also leaping away. This is not a strategic withdrawal, this is full-blown balls-to-the-wall getting the hell out of there. Against someone this good, you leap away, buy yourself distance, and immediately regroup your defenses from outside his range. Break contact and regroup!

If you ever see two guys tie it up and suddenly one leaps back but still has a look of ferocity on his face, what you are looking at is two good fighters. The guy ain't running; he just broke contact to keep from being taken down. The fight isn't even close to being over; in fact, it's probably going to get worse because they now have each other's measure. A good fighter will sacrifice the problems of closing the distance again in order to escape getting into a trap's point of no return. This springing away is risky, but hanging around and being slammed onto your head is worse.

Again, I cannot stress enough that a major point to understand about how these things work is knowing where the actual danger is. These moves generally are made up of two aspects. One is the grip itself. The part that is the real danger, though, is the motion of his arm! It is here that he positions *your* arm in a danger zone. These motions are designed to take you to the limits of your limb's flexibility and ability to turn

What makes this so effective is when someone touches

you, you focus on the actual touch or grip. While you are focusing on that, the person is maneuvering your arm into a position where the slack is taken out. Your limbs can only turn so far in certain directions. Once all the flex and twist is taken out, you are left with one of two choices—either resist and get bones broken or literally throw yourself onto your head.

Whatever you do, break the grip immediately. In doing so you are destroying the maneuvering of your arm. The draw is the most surefire way to escape, but the lever, twist, and punch also work real well. Often the best way to get out of the trap is head in the direction he wants you to go. But do it faster than he intended. In doing so you arrive at the place he wants you to be, but you still have slack and flexibility in your limb when you get there. At this point you keep going beyond where he wanted you. This is the blowing through the trap that I was talking about. You showed up where he wanted you to be but two hours early and at a hundred miles an hour. The trap was designed for you to be chugging along at thirty miles an hour and when he was ready for you. It ain't gonna work this time, Blue.

• • • • • •

Everything in this chapter is designed to keep you from going to the floor. What I've covered here are the basics. You have to go out and practice them with your buddies. All the throws and grips that I've ever encountered can be messed up if you move in time. The trick is to figure out a move's early warning signs and short-out the process before it can get sufficiently advanced. It's important for you to not only practice a move but to get to the point where you can instinctively identify what your opponent is trying to do. If you practice these basics, you can foil most of what you will encounter out there—if and only if you can identify what's coming. If you're practicing and drilling, pay attention to what it feels like to be tossed while your partner is tossing you. In time you'll be able to identify the early stages of a move immediately. From then on, practice breaking free from that point. If someone grabs you in certain places, you will know instinctively what you need to do to fuck up his move.[6]

# FOOTNOTES

[1] This same attitude led me to support my toy habit from the Mattel toy company (formerly based in Hawthorne, California) by finding a way to get to their seconds Dumpster through the city's flood control system. The Dumpster was buried deep in the complex and unreachable by going over the fence (many a local kid had tried). Like rats in the night, we'd swarm out of the drainage pipes to grab factory-seconds toys and disappear before the patrol came back (7 minutes, 30 seconds between patrols).

[2] If you kick the shit out of a guy, his ego will be hurt, but not enough to prevent him from suing you and the company you're working for. On the other hand, if you trip him and he falls on his ass, he's not as likely to try court action. Nobody is really sure if you tripped him, while everyone saw you punch him. Besides, he was drunk at the time, and everyone knows that drunks fall down. (Unless it's for your benefit, always leave the witnesses unaware or confused.)

[3] Also the inventor of the AK-1, known today as a fist-size rock suitable for throwing.

[4] A rock climbing term for such a solid grip that you could set up camp, cook dinner, read the paper, and watch some TV while hanging on. It might as well be a handle it's so good.

[5] A thrust off from your far leg as you accidently sever his spinal cord with his nose helps this process immensely. Not only does it commit your body weight to the strike (which, incidentally, is striking equilaterally to his stance integrity), it closes the distance, which screws up this move.

⁶ A freebie is that most formally trained martial artists freeze in shock when a move goes wrong. This is because they don't train to screw up each other's moves. He's expecting you to do what was practiced in the dojo, not an unexpected sneaky.

# 3 ▼ Spoiling the Dance

*"Misery no longer loves company. These days it demands it."*
—From a conversation regarding the state of life

The look of horror on the guy's face was priceless as he realized that something was seriously wrong. He was faced with the awful truth that he had a choice—either follow me to the floor or lose his left ear along with a clot of hair. He opted for retaining both ears. Once we hit the ground, the fact that he was bigger than me sort of lost its advantage. Later, I was sitting there quietly listening to a guy named Manuel describe to a group what I had done to the guy. He hadn't noticed that I was there until he turned to me and said, "You should have seen it." With a straight face I replied, "I did." Manuel did a double take as he recognized me. "Yeah, you probably did see it, didn't you?" he fired off without missing a beat. I gotta hand it to Manuel, he was quick on the recovery.[1]

What that guy hadn't realized on that day long ago in junior high school was that even back then, I was committed to taking anyone who threw me down with me. It had been nearly three years since my brother had joined the wrestling team, and I had learned a lot. The most important thing I had learned was, if I was going down, I was taking company. Later I added making sure that I landed in the better position and my opponent in the unqualified worse one.

There are four points to achieving these goals: 1) somehow dragging your opponent down with you, 2) twisting so he lands on the bottom and you on top, 3) strategically placing elbows and knees so your landing is the most painful event possible to your opponent, and 4) making sure that he doesn't return the favor. (Number four came about a few years later when I dragged someone over and had it all lined up to land with an elbow in his bread basket, only to discover that he had longer arms than me. Worse, he had beaten me to the finish line by getting his arm into position. I damn near got skewered on the guys elbow. Ooowww!)

Truthfully speaking, you now have all the basic ingredients to achieve these goals. You picked them up in Chapter 2. It's now just a matter of applying them in a different situation. What works here are the centerline/pivot, the horizontal roll, sticking your limb out, and tumbling. Sounds simple doesn't it? It is.

## LANDING ON TOP

So let's look at how you might end up in a situation needing these nasties. Okay, there you are minding your own business, just punching somebody out. Suddenly this guy decides that he doesn't like your long-distance affection any more, and he rushes you to give you a big, wet, sloppy kiss. His sudden burst of passion results in both of you falling to the floor. As long as Ms. Manners isn't around to advise you what to do in this sort of sticky situation, let me offer a few suggestions . . .

It's real common for someone to try to tackle you when he begins to lose the fight. If you have stance integrity/mobility and remember to pivot, you can often knock the guy down by deflecting his rush. If, on the other hand, you've gotten a little sloppy with the footwork, you're now in the risk zone of being elected to shine the floor with your ass.[2] It is at this point that you should begin to consider who gets to be on top. (Ever wonder where that term "coming out on top" came from?)

The trick of either taking your thrower down with you or making sure he ends up on bottom consists of two parts: a solid grip and adding your own extra energy into the equation. It's the energy thing we're going to examine first. The most common way of doing this is through a twist.

When that buster tackles you, what you have to do is give up trying to hold him back.[3] Gather him unto your bosom. Get his ass point-blank range with you. I'm talking about dragging him into chest-to-chest position. There are four reasons why you want to do this: 1) It's easier to flip him onto the bottom from this point. This has to do with physics, time, speed, and size. 2) You can control the fall to make sure who lands in the worse position. This has to do with body weight instead of muscle doing your work for you. 3) You can place your elbows and knees for the landing. This has to do with you hurting him. 4) You can effectively prevent him from doing the same. This has to do with making sure he doesn't hurt you.

Where most people screw the pooch on this one is as they go over, they're still trying to break away from the guy, either by escaping or pushing him off. This interferes with the twist and fall process. They wait too long to start a spin. At this point, most people get this stupid "oh shit" expression and just hang on for the ride. When they hit, they're on the bottom. Ouch! Truth of the matter is, there is only so much time before you're going to meet the ground. This is a bottom-line, unalterable fact that cuts across all other concerns. In that time you'd better act fast.

Somewhere in that time you're going to cruise past what? The "point of no return." Remember this? It's when you know you're going to be going over so you abandon your attempts to stay up and prepare for landing. From that point to when you hit the ground is all the time that you have to ensure that numb nuts plays landing pad. Let's say a half second was lost in the rush/tackle. The period of time between you and the floor is now going to be something less than a second. Resist only to that point if it's a slow fall. If it's a fast fall, you can usually sense when you are going too fast to keep from blasting past that point. "No way to stop in time, better prepare for impact." Once you hit that point or know that you're going to go screaming past it in the near future, you start twisting. Accept that you're going to hit ground early and you can usually counter any advantage that the guy might gain from it. Take a look at the illustration.

Now for you would-be physics majors, I have a question. Going the same speed, which ball would it take longer for point A to rotate around to where point B is?

Exactly—the bigger one is slower. This is because of its larger circumference. Now let's say that the process is going to be interrupted after 1 second. The small ball would be able to accomplish the rotation, while the large one would be stopped with A and B where points C are now.

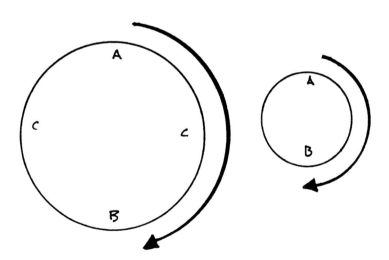

Where all of this comes home is that the interruption is going to be the ground. Instead of the bigger ball impacting on point A, it's going to hit on the side. If you are point B and your attacker point A, by landing on your side you both get nailed. Instead of him landing on you, you both slam into the ground. Now while B is going to take less direct impact than it would have before, it's still going to hurt.

While twisting so you both take equal impact is preferable to him landing on you—and you may have to settle for it in a pinch—what you really want to do is get that full rotation and land on top of him. The way to accomplish this is to drag him close so you both are a smaller ball. When you do this, your twist is more likely to put him on the ground first than you both hitting simultaneously. If you're holding him out at arm's length, the distance you'll need to travel is too great in the time you have.

The second part, the issue about controlling the fall, is simple. It has to do with body weight being moved. Remember, to get him to be the skid mark, you have to move not only your body weight but his. When you are twisting, you are moving your body weight. An ungrounded, equal or near-equal body weight in motion is more likely to be affected by an equal force and mass. (It's gonna take something that's just as big and moving just as fast to blow it off course. This means it's gonna take your body weight to move his.) This is where body to body contact comes in. If you try to hold him out at arm's length, you're less likely to be able to control the fall because your arms aren't able to effectively transfer the energy of your body's momentum in this situation. You no longer have the earth's leverage behind your motion, and there's too much flex in your extended arm. All of which is a fancy way of saying that you won't be able to throw the guy around where you want him if you're holding him out at arm's length.

You really don't want to end up on the bottom of a bum's rush or tackle. It's likely that there are going to be things lying on the ground that would be painful to impact against. This, in combination with not wanting his body weight landing on top of you to further complicate the situation, is why you will be wanting to land on top. A beer bottle usually breaks from the weight of one person landing on it; two people bouncing off it is definitely going to break it. Also, if there are furniture and walls around that he was intending to have you inspect at close range, it is only proper that he go first. While the Marquis de Queensbury may not have made it to the streets, "After you, my dear Alphonse!" is always in order.

Another real good thing about closing the distance is damn near nobody knows how to punch from that close. Once you hit the floor, forget punching—you can't get your body weight behind it. With him tied up close, he's not going to be able to punch you effectively either. By the time he shifts gears to a new attack mode, you'll have been there for awhile. (We'll get into point-blank viciousness you can do while on the floor later on in the book.)

Where most people mess up on this one is that they glom on with their arms and leave their asses hanging way the

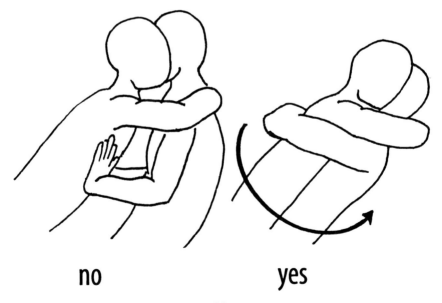

no          yes

hell out there. If you close with someone, make sure that your entire body is glued to the guy. If you're glued tight, you're less likely to break something in the fall. But you have to do it in such a way that there are no rigid angles, like your elbows sticking out, for you to land on and break, and you should be aware of and avoid *his* rigid angles (e.g., his shoulder) landing on your arm. All in all, it's a situational call whether to ride him to the floor or get your arms out of there.

Don't leave your ass hanging out in the boondocks and just hang on with your upper body. If you do, it's only going to take the guy a second to realize that while he can't hit you effectively around the head, he can still knee you in the balls with force. Another nasty about grabbing someone wrong is if you pin his arms down by only grabbing his shoulder, he can shift to uppercuts to your body. It is one of the few punches you can throw effectively from the ground. If you're having trouble taking a shot to the face, an uppercut is really going to ruin your day. Just know that you're not going to be unarmed when the fight gets that close.

## IMPACTING WITH ELBOWS AND KNEES

As you're tumbling around ass over tea kettle, you might want to consider adding a few things to the equation. If on your downward trip you should happen to check your watch to see what time it is, this usually places your elbow in either his chest or bread basket. While being caught between the impact of hitting the floor and your own weight slamming into him will probably rattle him a good one, you can improve the situation by a strategically placed elbow. Your weight crashing into him in a focalized point is much worse than you just landing on him. If you can't get your elbow up to his short ribs or diaphragm in time, landing with your shoulder in his chest is almost as much fun.

Knees are also really effective. Even if you miss the most dreaded of all targets, having your body weight focused in your knee and slamming it into someone's thigh will give him a limp like you'd not believe. What you have to watch out for is making sure you don't miss and accidentally hit the ground with your knee. That hurt? It looked real painful . . .

I personally recommend keeping away from head butts in the actual falling part. There's too much wild kinetic energy around to do it safely. You're just as likely to knock yourself out as you are your opponent. You're both lying there unconscious on the floor, and it's up to the crowd to decide what to do with you. Once you're on the floor, though, a properly applied head butt will not only drive the guy's nose through the back of his head, it will drive the fans wild.

If you can arrange it, it is best to land on your side on top of someone. Not only does it drive your shoulder and hip into the person, but it seriously lessens the likelihood of you landing on a knee or elbow. Another goody about this is you can, if the situation allows, continue the motion into a vertical roll after you've hit the floor. This is assuming that the guy is so shocked by this unexpected landing situation that he loosens his grip (this happens a lot). A combination of impacts, both floor and you, and your unexpected twisting can easily put you in a position to roll away.

If you can do it immediately after impact, you can use the energy of the "bounce" to help your roll. Once you hit, you shift your direction and use the energy of the impact to spring away. It takes some practice with your tumbling and falling to be able to do this, but it's not as difficult as it may sound. Also, there are some seriously nasty physics involved which I won't bore you with, but it hurts him more. Something along the same lines as the cat using your dick as a launch pad.

Another thing about this is it allows you to roll free of the tangle of arms and legs and regain your feet. Remember law number 4—get up immediately. Just because you now have the tools to have so much fun on the way down doesn't mean you want to stay there. Not only may the guy have friends who won't be on your side, but you standing and him on the floor is definitely to your advantage. Besides, floor fighting gets your clothes dirty. We may not all be able to look like James Bond after a fight, but one should make the attempt.

The process by which you bring your knees and elbows into alignment during a fall should sweep any other players from the field. As you bring in your nasties, you sweep his arms and legs out of the way. The trick behind this is that you don't use your arm/leg muscles to do it. What you have to do is tuck or lock your limb into position (with arms and an occasional leg position, it's tight against your body) and use your body weight as the mover. This makes it so your weight is behind your arms and legs. You're not relying on the muscles in your arms to sweep the field clear—your body weight is moving the opposition.

Tuck your elbow to your side, fist near your shoulder, and lock it in place. Now turn your body so the same shoulder comes forward. With your arm locked it becomes an unmovable carrier of your body weight. Now instead of doing it fast, tighten the muscles of your body and turn all at once in the same manner. That arm becomes a bulldozer blade, with your body being the bulldozer. Any unlocked limb is going to be blown away in the face of this action. It's your body weight vs. his arm's muscle—no contest. This also positions your limbs in a perfect place for them to be used as springs to help you get back up.

Another advantage to landing on your side is your opponent may be a millisecond later than you at getting an elbow in place, but it can still happen. Either intentionally or accidentally, he might still manage to get an elbow up there to welcome you. The process of twisting on your side not only increases the chances of you sweeping the field of these problems, but it lessens the target you're presenting against any latecomers. Unless you're a serious fan of down-home cooking (or love your beer), most people are wider than they are deep. This means that more often than not, any unexpected elbow or knee will only manage to get a glancing shot. As anyone who has ever played baseball will tell you, it's hard to hit a small moving circular object exactly head on. A glancing blow will actually end up directing your energy for your escape.

I do have to warn you, though, you should reserve the nasties I've described in these last few paragraphs regarding elbows and shoulders to the chest for serious shindigs— ones where you know the guy is trying to seriously hurt or kill you. It is possible to kill someone with these. You land just right and you can not only break bones but drive ribs into hearts and lungs. If it's a friendly drunken brawl at a party, you don't want to really damage the guy beyond making sure that you land on top of him. Of course, a knee to the groin is all in good clean fun.

## ROLLING WITH IMPACT

Not overly long ago I was teaching a Level 1 knife class to a group at a particular dojo. I have to admit, the dojo owner had tried to cram too many people into a small area. It wasn't the size of the class I objected to; it was the limited space. I learned a serious lesson from that incident, and I now have standards of student/space ratios. I was amazed at how much trouble people were having not only running into each other but handling it when it happened.

The fact that my assistant and I were walking behind people who were drilling in a limited space meant that we got bumped into and stepped on a lot. The thing was, we weren't even coming close to getting hurt. I also noticed something else. I watched two people slam into each other and I realized that while I had taught them to pivot, they were only applying it to face-to-face contact.

I stopped the class and had them line up. "How many people here have run into me?" I asked. About half of the class raised their hands. I asked the same question regarding my assistant. About three-quarters of the class had either stepped on or run into us during a weekend of practice. "Did you notice with all of that, we're not hurt?" The class muttered assent. "Why?" I asked.

After a few minutes of dead silence broken by an occasional "I dunno," someone suggested "because you're trained fighters." I nearly cried. Finally I told them, "The reason we haven't been hurt is because we've been rolling with the impact!" They looked at me like I had grown another head. I took a deep breath and explained that the pivot (which was the first thing that they had been taught) also works when you're struck from the side.

For the next 20 minutes I had them practice rolling off an impact from the side. Group A body checked group B. The lights went on inside many a head that the pivot works in circle and from all directions. The problem I guess is that every person in that dojo had been formally trained in hard-style martial arts. It was leading them to take a rooted stance against an impact and try to resist it. The idea of rolling with and away from an impact was totally foreign to these people. When I felt that they had a handle on it, we returned to the scheduled instruction. While people still ran into each other, there were no more problems with it. Since that time, rolling away from a side impact has been incorporated into my classes as a fundamental issue.

The reason I bring this incident up is to drive home a serious point. Not only during a fight, but during life in general, you're probably going to get slammed into from the side (or back). Often this entails getting knocked on your ass. You have to roll with it to avoid being hurt.

Not overly long ago I got plowed into as I was kneeling down looking for something on a lower shelf in a store. I was sent flying ass over end by a 17-year-old female who was in the middle of a fight with her boyfriend. She had tried to run from him and slammed into me. I was lying on the floor as she was screaming "get away from me" at lover boy. I considered getting bent about it, but I figured the guy had enough problems on his hands as it was. I had rolled with the impact and wasn't hurt. All that had happened to me was my dignity had been compromised. Shit, back in my hard-core drinking days, I'd done worse to it without any outside help. Besides, the girl was so upset at him that she didn't even see me, which was no mean feat since we were lying on the floor next to each other.

In life in general, all I gotta say is "shit happens." You're going to get plowed into by people. If you know how to roll with it you'll minimize the damage you'll take. This is from the front, side, and back. If you're not hurt, you can make a rational decision whether to get pissed off or not. If you get hurt during a fall, it's damn near guaranteed that you're going to get mad. If you avoid a painful landing, you'll probably still be annoyed, but you can look to see what's going on. If it's not an attack on you personally, you may want to seriously consider not getting involved.

Since I wasn't hurt I could assess the situation calmly. The couple, of whom one half had plowed into me, were too wrapped up in their own problems to notice what was going on outside their particular dance. People do that—they fixate on their own problems to the exclusion of the outside. In order for them to notice me, I would have had to become a problem of a bigger magnitude than what they were involved in. I'll tell you the truth, that chick was so focused on her boyfriend she would not have recognized me as a threat until I busted her nose. That is literally the magnitude of the energy you need to intrude on a domestic argument.

Especially with a domestic fight, you have to remember that you are dealing with a unit. That's two people, not just one. Therefore, what happens to them must be as a unit— both get equal shares. They both get bounced, they both get told to shut up, or, if it erupts, they both get their heads kicked in. It's been my experience that a man will recognize an outside threat faster than a woman in the middle of a domestic fight. However a woman will nail you from behind while you're hashing out with the man faster than a man will. I'll leave why that is to the anthropologists, sociologists, and psychologists to argue about. But I will warn you not to focus your attention on only one person. Often both partners will turn on you. While they may have been ready to kill each other before you interrupted, now they will gladly aim that same energy at you. While you're dealing with one, the other is winding up with a brick.

If it isn't a domestic fight but another type of situation, you'd better still assess if you want to get involved. If you feel that you must join the party, I recommend that you wait until the immediate dance is over before joining the festivities. Say, for example, two guys are about to go at it. Two's company, three's a crowd. The logistics of a three-way fight are really bizarre, and I recommend you keep away from it for a few reasons. Let them fight first, then you kick the shit out of the winner. Of course, this also allows you time to correctly assess the magnitude of the situation. You might discover that this fight was settled by one of the members pulling a weapon and scrubbing his opponent. In situations like that, you may want to reconsider arguing with the winner.

It is an odd dynamic that a third party entering an equation will often be the one that the weapon is used on first. I've known more than a few people who've gotten seriously hurt, some who were killed, for interrupting at the wrong time. It has to do with the fact that there is a recognizable step-by-step process of violence. You can interfere in the early stages (pre -n determined). If you step into it when the shit is hot, you're likely to get your dick bit off. I'm dead serious here. If someone has just knocked someone over into you, you can bet your huevos that the shit is hot.

The only way to safely intervene in the hot spot of a fight is by having major backup and falling on the whole thing like a ton of lead. This is overwhelming the intensity of the fight with a much more powerful force. No talking, just serious hammering. Two guys fighting suddenly have five gorillas land on them. It's been my experience that the only way a single third party can safely break up a hot fight is by busting a chair over both contestants' heads. This is the same thing as five guys doing a blitzkrieg on the scufflers.

Watch bouncers on this one. Usually they work in groups, but if the guy is alone, either he is going to step on the situation before it explodes or take down the winner. Nobody in his right mind jumps into the middle of a hot fight alone.[4]

I've been plowed into from behind both intentionally and unintentionally. If you can't manage to grab ahold of the person slamming into you, and often you can't in unexpected situations, roll the hell out of the way. If it is a case of someone plowing into you and you both going down, you can roll enough that he goes one way and you go another. If it's an attack, he's probably not going to expect you to fall and roll away. If he's expecting you to fall in front of him, he's likely to hesitate when you roll. Not only do you buy yourself the time it will take him to close the distance again, but you often get an extra second of him standing there wondering what went wrong.

This conforms to the second rule of floor fighting—buy yourself distance. This is especially necessary if it is an attack. Often the guy will simply shove you from behind to knock you over. You on the ground and him standing immediately over you is not a situation you want to be in. Any situation where you can't grab on, practice rolling away. If it is an attack, by rolling away you can counter his advantage of getting the drop on you. If it's something else, you can make up your mind if you want to get involved or not.

Whatever you do, *don't fight the energy!* That's the best way to get hurt! Go out and practice jostling with your friends to get the hang of rolling away from an impact. After you get some experience tumbling, your body will begin to know instinctively what to do when it is faced with losing balance. This ability of rolling with the energy and not landing hard is the most important aspect of floor fighting. If you're hurt during the landing, you've lost the fight! If it's a stomping rather than a fight, you're fucked if you land hard. That's because your opponent won't hesitate if you slam into the ground as planned. While you're trying to recover from the first shock, he's going to press his advantage by kicking your ribs in. Remember, real fights are more like assaults—one guy gets the immediate advantage and exploits it. Your being hurt during a fall is the "immediate advantage" he needs.

## CLOSING
Actually, that last paragraph pointed out something that I think needs detailing. I did say that one of the laws of floor fighting is to buy yourself distance. In case you haven't noticed, this chapter has been teaching you how to keep close instead of gaining distance. What's this? Has Animal put his foot in his mouth? While I do that occasionally, I'm not quite doing it here.

Let me sketch out some parameters here. If you are down on the ground and your opponent is standing, it is a categorically bad situation. You don't want to be there. Maybe if you've studied certain obscure forms of Shao-lin kung fu for 20 years or fighting on a sheet of ice, you might be able to turn it to your advantage, but I'm betting that you're not likely to be filling those qualifications any time soon. In short, I'm writing for where you are now. In 999 times out of 1,000, the guy still on his feet has the advantage. That thousandth time is when the guy who got knocked over uses the moment of freedom to draw his gun and shoot the standing guy. Now we know what we're dealing with here. It is up to you to immediately neutralize any advantage that the guy might gain by putting you down.

If you find yourself on the floor, the best thing to do is to get up. That way the threat is neutralized. But here's the problem—unless you do something to put your attacker on hold, getting up is just as dangerous as going down. You have to do something so your opponent can't attack you during this process. In any situation, the safest way to get up is to buy yourself distance. If you are out of the guy's reach, it is physically impossible for him to interfere. The second way to ensure your safety while getting up is to stun him and use that time to get up. However, the best way by far to ensure your safety is a combination of the two.

How you do it is mostly situational. However, I can with confidence born of experience state that if the guy ends up on the ground with you, it's going to be harder for him to prevent you from getting up. If you take your attacker down with you (and land properly), you can use his recovery time to roll away and get back up. This actually makes sure that the third law of "regroup your offense/defenses" has been met before going for the safety of distance to regain your feet. In this case, your closing with him is a defensive action, the results of which will aid you in your gaining distance. It can be used as the final shot before you break contact and continue mission, or the ingredient you need for finishing the fight in your favor.

What we're talking about is shuffling priorities here. Sometimes law three plays first; other times law two is immediate. As funny as this may sound, a flow chart works well here. Furthermore it works in nearly any situation that I'm going to cover in this book. Observe the flow chart at the top of the next page.

### DEALING WITH TRAINED THROWERS

Now we're going to shift over from the "Amateur Hour" and look at how to handle someone who *does* know how to throw you properly. I'll tell you the truth—against a person trained in throwing or grappling techniques, it's real hard not to get tossed on your head. The way to handle one of these people is to be so balanced and flexible that you never allow them an opportunity to unbalance you (yeah, right). Okay, failing that, the way to handle this situation is to take control of your own flight path and invite them to come along. The trick here is still adding energy to the equation. Once again, I'm going to mention the "blowing your way

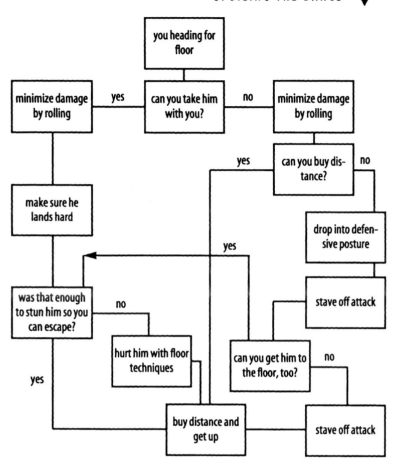

through a trap" routine. It sounds crazier than hell to just say it this way, but the best way to fuck up a throw is to leap into it. The trick is to throw yourself in the right direction.

The way a throw works is that your thrower is moving your energy/weight in a certain direction (usually unexpected). The most common ways to do this is a combination of joint locks (which we've discussed already) and moving body weights (yours and his). A trained thrower will move his entire body weight and drag you with him in the direction of his choice. What you are faced with is his entire body weight hauling your ass in a particular direction. If that direction is toward a table or wall, you can be in some serious shit.

On the arm throws, he's either used up or locked out your arm's flexibility during the process of the throw. That means all the shock-absorbing qualities of the arm are removed. When the extent of your arm is reached, it becomes like a tow chain which will drag you along. What the thrower is doing in these cases is literally towing you in the direction he wants you to go. In some throws, by locking your arm instead of towing, you are pushed along by that locked limb. The same physics apply in body grip throws. In these cases, however, it's *his* arms that are locked for energy transfer.

Most of the throwing styles work in a particular geometric form—the circle. It is their greatest strength, but it is also the way out of most of their moves. Most throws are based in moving in a circular manner around a straight-line attack (a straight punch, for instance). Look at the diagram at right.

The first is a general assessment of a situation. A straight line of attack is avoided by slipping in a circular manner to the side. Now look at the second picture of that same line of attack and the line of stance integrity of the attacker.[5] By moving off the direct line of attack, the defender has moved into a position that is exactly 90 degrees off the attacker's line of stance integrity. You know what that means . . . somebody is going to hit the floor!

The trick of many throws is to shift position so the thrower's body weight is in the area equilateral to the line of stance integrity. The combination of the irresistible pull of the person's entire weight dragging or shoving you in that direction is what will plant your snot locker in the dirt.

What that person is doing is taking your energy and mass that were moving one way and, by adding his in a way that you're least stable, redirecting where your energy (hence mass) is going. This is known locally as "using your own movement against you." Sooner or later, gravity is

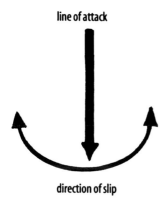

line of attack

direction of slip

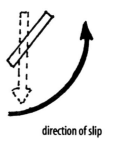

line of stance integrity

direction of slip

line of attack

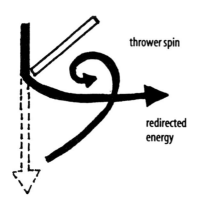

thrower spin

redirected energy

original course

going to put in its two cents and you're going to start falling. The real circle of a throw is here.

What that person has done is use that center-line pivot against you! By muckling[6] onto your arm or shirt, he has used the force of his body spinning around that pivot to throw you through a window. The major trick to most throws is that they really are an orbital sling. You are orbiting that person's centerline/ pivot until he lets go of you. Once released of the orbit, you're going to return to a straight flight path. Science fiction writers talk about using a planet's orbit to sling spaceships into space all the time. When you break free from an orbit, you're going to be going balls to the wall in whatever direction you're heading. He's either going to use that sling to slam you into a wall/object or he's going to do a downward spiral that will plow you into the ground!

I say fuck it! Turn around is fair play. If he's going to use you as an orbiting asteroid, I say that you decide when you want to go bye-bye! He wants you to go to Neptune, you hang on until you're heading for Mercury! Let him deal with the fact that for every action there is an equal and opposite reaction! So what if it happens that the blowback is in the place that is equilaterally opposed to his stance integrity! He can dish it out, but can he take it?! *Hah!*

What happens in situations like this is that in order for him to keep his balance, he must either let you go at a certain point or only go so far in a particular direction. If he fails to meet either of these conditions, the very forces that he set in motion will turn against him. So what are you waiting for? Help him along!

When you were a short squirt, did you ever play a game where you and your friend held onto each other's hands and spun around? The object (aside from getting sick) was to spin off each other's energy. You'd pick up speed until centrifugal force threw you apart and either onto your head or into the bushes. The same physics apply here.

his intended
direction for you

new and improved

94

I've already mentioned breaking a grip to prevent joint locking when it comes to dealing with these guys. However, another aspect of breaking a grip is that it allows you to glom on to whoever is throwing you. While the shirt/jacket/chest/shoulder is preferable, any handy appendage or portion of anatomy will do. As you're flying by, you slap a gorilla grip on the sucker and get ready for the shit to hit the fan. This is a serious "oh shit" situation for the guy. Suddenly he's no longer in control of your departure time. Instead of your being in orbit around him, now you're both in orbit around each other. The pivot point has shifted from inside him to somewhere between your two bodies. In case you didn't realize it, back then the reason you quit doing that game as a kid was because it fucking hurts!

If you hang on long enough, you will rotate around to a place where his stance integrity is shot to hell. Suddenly he's got the same physics that messed you up in the first place. Instead of being thrown, however, he's got you hanging on out at the end of his arm kicking and screaming. Your weight is going to drag him over onto his face. Remember, your job is not to make this guy's life easy.

What you really want to do is to enclose his circle in a bigger circle of your own. Instead of going where he wants you to go, you curl around him and keep going around in the orbit. This usually results in his being slung out of orbit, both of you going down in a tangle of arms and legs, or, more likely, a combination of the two.

Now if you really want to move up in status to that state which my bro so eloquently claimed I was capable, you can add in your own booster rockets. Instead of just going along passively, step on his foot that's on the accelerator. Leap into it. Not only does this allow you a better chance of being able to pick your landing place by overshooting what he had in mind, but by speeding up the process, you leave him less time to adjust to the new situation. Most people expect one of two responses in these situations. The first is that you attempt to resist. As explained many a time, against his body weight, futile gesture. Nonetheless, the most common reaction. The second most common reaction is to allow yourself to be led along without resistance to the point of no return. Since people don't recognize the threat, they don't fight it.

What throwers don't expect is for you to scream "BANZAI!" and not only dive into a move, but drag them with you. Once you're on the floor together, it's an equal fight again. (Actually, after reading this book, it may not be. Yer gonna moider da bum.)

One of my personal favorites for dealing with someone who throws you over his leg is to lock your knee at a 90-degree angle as you go flying by. His leg is there to make sure that you go horizontal by knocking your legs out from under you. What he's doing is only taking part of your energy against his leg; not enough to blow his leg out of the way, but enough to trip you. By locking your leg in a position that acts as a snag, you can usually end up taking that guy's leg with you. Why not? Your body weight is behind the throw; he's relying on only catching part of that weight on his leg. If unexpectedly your entire body weight is slamming into the back of his knee, he's going to join you on the ground. I'm renowned for slamming my knee into the back of other people's knees.

The major thing you have to keep in mind about these kinds of maneuvers, though, is to watch how you land. As I mentioned previously, if you can go out and find a gymnastics instructor, you'll be doing yourself a major favor. The hardest part about diving into a throw is making sure that you don't land on your head and break your neck. That added leap is to make sure you have enough juice to land in a forward or shoulder roll below your neck. You land across your shoulders. Actually if you remember what I said and practice popping back up enough to compensate for dojo training, you might be able to get away with learning how to tumble from a martial arts school. Starting

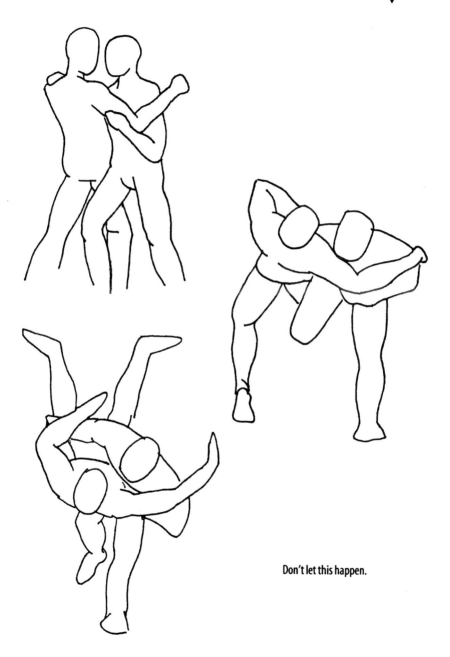

Don't let this happen.

*Taking thrower down with a knee hook.*

out with a gymnast is better, though, as they really stress protecting your head and neck.

Another important safety tip here is that, since you are tangled up with the guy, the odds are you really won't be able to pop back up immediately. In fact, there exists the strong possibility that the guy might land on you. If I were a nice guy, I'd tell you the most you can do is minimize the damage of hitting the ground by rolling. However, by now it is not news to you that I can be a vicious little mother-fucker. Therefore I heartily recommend that you make sure that if the guy is going to land on you, his landing pad consists of your elbow, shoulder, or knee.

At the same time that you are extending points of interest to your company, you should also be keenly aware of him doing the same to you. Remember the third law—regroup your offense/defense. Him throwing you and you dragging him down can neutralize the threat, but him falling onto an elbow into the diaphragm definitely means he's getting the worst of the deal.

## FOOTNOTES

[1] I should also point out that Manuel was not only smaller than me, he was one of the few people who could out wrestle me in our grade and weight class. Where I had one bigger brother, he had five to practice with. Not only was he the youngest, but he was the runt of the litter. This made him pure hell to tangle with.

[2] Actually, even if you're good with your footwork, you can still be tackled. Look at William Cheung and the story I told you about in the beginning of this book.

[3] You will note I said, "*when* he tackles you." You can pivot and shed an attempted tackle, but if he gets too close and it looks like it's going to succeed, time to change the dance to the grab and twist.

[4] The bartender with a shotgun still conforms to this equation. It is the equivalent of the chair over the heads, but from a safer distance. Suddenly, there is no question as to whom the bigger force is. Unless you want to become part of the pattern on the wallpaper, you chill out when someone has the drop on you with a shotgun.

⁵ Stance integrity is the stability and strength of a stance to resist a force from a particular angle. Since we only have two feet, no matter how we place them, there will be a straight line between them. From this line up to a 45-degree angle off from it is an area of "stance integrity," which can take an impact or force and often withstand the pressure. However, a force from 45 degrees upward to 135 degrees will often result in you being knocked over. There's more to it than

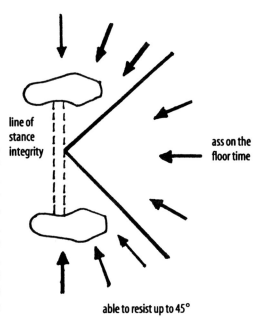

that, but that's the gist of it. I cover this quite extensively in my knife videos. It really is incredibly important to understand and use during a fight.

⁶ Muckle, by the way, is what something with claws does. A lobster won't grab you, it'll muckle on to you.

# ▼4 FLOOR WORK

*"What is past is prologue."*
—William Shakespeare, *The Tempest*

It was a nice sunny day. June in California is usually a beautiful time of the year, time to sit back and relax. I was lying on my back in the middle of a green field under the bright blue sky trying to keep a psychotic from sticking a sword through my crotch. While I have been accused occasionally of not having all the batting in my attic, I know for sure that many of my old running buddies had elevators that didn't reach the top floor.

In light of the lack of normal restraints that my friends and I had a habit of showing in certain situations, combined with the fact that one of these same people was trying to play "Sword in the Stone" with my nuts using a double-handed bastard sword, it was rather important that I not leave any holes in my defense. I was busily concentrating on the intricate patterns being woven in the air twixt legs and sword. In short, I was giving it all I had.

It had started out as a quiet little intimate four-way melee. The Foss brothers were both down, and I was looking to see that my partner had not been hurt too badly when Matthew (that same bastard from Chapter 1) did an overhanded slam from behind with his sword. In return for this action, I turned around and proceeded to imitate a can opener with an attitude.

As often happens in those sort of dances, we clenched up. He took the opportunity to heel hook me and blast me over. As I slammed into the ground, my sword flew out of my hand with the impact. In civilized circles, this would have ended the bout. We'd heard about this thing called civilized behavior, but we didn't believe it for a minute. With that damn maniacal expression of glee, he leapt forward and proceeded to try to skewer my cajones. This was a situation I had every intention of preventing. Needless to say, the next few minutes were a study in complete concentration. He'd thrust or chop and I'd kick the blade aside.

Finally he made the mistake of getting too close, and I blew his leg out with a side kick. He came crashing down next to me, and he too lost his sword on impact. He fell head to foot with me. I attempted to scramble up and get my sword, but he grabbed onto me. I kicked him in the face to let him know how happy I was about that development. He thought that was a marvelous idea and returned the favor as he himself tried to get back up. Getting kicked in the face with a pair of bear paws solerets (flat-toed foot armor) pissed me off considerably, and I punched him in the crotch. The fact that I was wearing a clam shell gauntlet added a little weight to that move. We both broke away and skittered over to the nearest weapon. Let me tell you, skittering on all fours in full plate armor isn't real easy. We got our weapons back and proceeded to hack wildly at each other until we ended up collapsing in exhaustion.

A friend of mine captured the whole episode on film. This time instead of one person saying it, three people told me that it was great choreographing. The reason it looked so good, I told them, was because I was seriously trying to keep my nuts from getting chopped off! I was in a really bad place for that episode.

It's odd that the two stories which best exemplify the laws of floor fighting come from the days when I was a young buck hanging out with a pack of sword-wielding wackos.[1] It was years later when I was talking with my partner from the security/bouncing biz that I asked him in all the years we had worked together had he ever seen me taken to the ground. He thought about it and said, "No, come to think of it, I never did."

"That's because I know better. It's dangerous down there," I said. Bizarre as they may be, the story that I began this chapter and Chapter 1 with are perfect examples of what you need to do to survive on the ground.

In this story, once I hit the ground I immediately dropped into law 3 of regroup your defense/offensive capabilities. Since I was still in range of immediate danger, my major goal was firstly defensive.[2] From the second I hit the ground until I was able to blow his leg out from under him, my only concern was my defense. It wasn't until he made the mistake of getting too close that I was able to counterattack. Once I got him onto the ground, I only engaged him long enough for me to escape. When he hit, I was trying to get the hell out of Dodge. Unfortunately, he hadn't been stunned enough by his fall for me to make my getaway. It was the shock of my trying to blow his nuts into a fine pink mist that gave me time to skeedaddle.

You will note that in both stories I was eventually able to counterattack. My attacks either bought me space to get up or brought my opponent down to my level. These are the main goals of your offensive moves. Nothing else— either get him away from you or knock his ass down. That's it, bottom line. Once either of these have been accomplished, you get the hell out of there immediately. None of this trying to knock him out from the floor with a devastating kick. No "once he's down, I'll wrestle him" bullshit. You do not continue the fight on the ground any longer than you have to. Break away and get back up!

## FLOOR FIGHTING RANGES

I have in my time seen a number of martial artists and so called self-defense teachers try to teach floor fighting. Some have blown it by teaching that once you take the guy down, you hang around and wrassle. No way, Jose. Once he hits the floor, too, it's hasta la bye-bye time. In my opinion, however, they've all blown it in one key area—range. What is the effective range of floor fighting? This is the key point that cuts across everything else. The reason I feel most people miss this question is because the answer is in two parts. Take a look at the illustration below.

Where most people drop the ball on this one is that they teach someone to try offensive moves in the defensive range. While this might work in the occasional blue moon, what usually happens is the person who tries this is left with his dick flapping in the wind and his opponent still standing and able to attack. That's because you don't have the leverage to do offensive moves way out in defensive range. The effective defensive range of floor fighting is farther out than the offensive range. Your defensive range extends out to the extent of your leg's reach. Your offensive range is actually only out to the area around your knees and elbows. I'll go into the whys and wherefores of this in a second, but right now the most important thing you need to do is get the

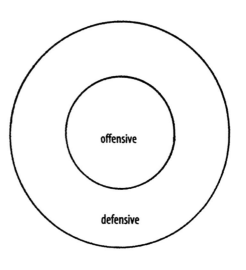

Floor fighting ranges.

104

idea of the two distances firmly dug into your gray matter.

Most of those fancy scissor sweeps and takedowns that people seem to love to teach just flat out will not fucking work past the offensive range. You try to take them out in defensive range and it's going to go to hell in a hand basket right quick. Not only do you not have the leverage to make it work, but you're short the reach to take both his legs into the infamous scissors. Not only will this not take the guy down, but it can easily result in you getting your legs broken with a stomp when you're left way out there with your ass swinging in the breeze.

## HITTING THE FLOOR

When you hit the floor, a number of things happen, most of them having to do with what you lose by being on the ground. Here's a detailed list of exactly what is wrong with being on the floor.

1) You lose mobility. Even if you roll instead of drag your ass over the floor, your ability to move effectively is seriously cut down.

2) Your options for quick motion is reduced to only two ways—rolling to left or to the right.

3) Your speed is seriously reduced. You cannot roll or crab nearly as fast as you can step.

4) If you are on your back, you can use either arm or leg to defend, but you cannot move from that position.[3]

5) If you go to one side, what you gain in mobility you lose by only having the limbs of one side available for blocking.

6) There is only one direction that is effective for defending. From every other direction you are exposed to attack.

7) You are extremely vulnerable to attacks from chairs, tables, etc. This is especially true of thrown objects.

8) It is a group dynamic that people will join in on stomping a downed person. While one guy may have thrown you, when you hit the ground spectators can and often do join in.

9) During the process of getting up, your balance is

compromised and your weight committed. This makes it extremely difficult to defend against any attack at this moment. You can get your ass kicked into next week and never have had a chance to block the attack.

All of these reasons are why you don't want to end up on the floor with your opponent still standing. If you're going down, either take that son of a bitch down with you or bounce back faster than a super ball. The same reasoning, however, is why you want your opponent on the floor. I don't care how good of a martial artist someone is, if I can get him onto the floor, a chair is going to settle the matter in my favor!

If you go down in a real fight, there isn't going to be anyone around to call a time out. I don't know about you, but I never really relied on the guy I was fighting having an overly developed sense of fair play and good sportsmanship. If I hit the floor, I expected him to try to press the advantage, and you better adopt that form of thinking if you want to make it out in the real world.

Most deaths by beatings occur at this point, where one guy is down and the stomp begins. He's down and everybody jumps in and starts kicking until the victim takes one shot too many and checks out. Even one guy can kick someone to death, so don't think that you're safe just because he's alone.

Now let's say that you agreed with everything I've said and diligently practiced rolling, tumbling, breaking grips, inviting company to the ground, etc. Nonetheless, you still end up on the ground with your opponent standing. Shit happens. He's pressing too hard for you to regain your feet or do anything immediately but defend. What do you do? It's time for floor work.

## COUNTERING

As I've mentioned earlier, don't concern yourself with counterattacking until he's in range. The thing about the defensive range is that you don't need your body weight to operate out there. In fact, the most important thing you need out there is speed. Unlike when you're on your feet, on the ground you've lost speed and mobility, and you have to get them back in some form or the other.

If you have ever read any other book by me, I hope that you've read one where I've talked about the advantages of countering and deflecting over straight-out blocking. The important safety tip about fighting from the floor is *you don't block!* You instead deflect and counter any attack. By definition, a block stops the energy of an attack. Well I have a question—on your feet, if a block doesn't work you can still roll with the punch. But on the floor, if a block doesn't work, where are you going to roll? You got no place to go! If it's a downward attack and you're on the ground, there's this thing behind you called Mother Earth. If she can handle airplanes plowing into her, do you think she's going to move out of the way for you? You blocking means you take the whole impact. Ker-fucking-splat! Let me tell you, bucko, lying on the ground is not the same thing as "grounding." If you try to block the infamous side attack (kick to the ribs), you're still going to take the energy. Great—you stop the kick by becoming a kickball.

Face it, nothing in the previous paragraph is a good scene to be in. Ninety-nine times out of a hundred, blocking is bad news when you are on the floor. There is one situation which you can "block" that I will be going into, but it is a special situation where you are positioned to be able to absorb impact.

A counter, on the other hand, doesn't try to stop the energy of your opponent's attack; it deflects it. It usually does this by altering the course of the attack. Usually this is done by getting in and messing up the process early or near its point of origin. Your defense on the floor has to be designed to deflect impacts from your body. A block is just taking the impact on another part of your body. If someone tries to stomp you, don't try to stop the force; simply knock it to the side where it will not do any damage, or short it out early before it picks up speed.

Often the sudden shift in resistance, impact, and timing will throw the guy off for a second. Counters are like a stick in the spokes of a moving bike or an expected resistance not being where it was supposed to be. Have you ever stepped down and expected a stair to be there that wasn't? That can seriously mess up your balance. It can work the same way with floor fighting.

By not relying on muscle to stop a blow, your arms and legs pick up speed. This begins to compensate for some of the speed you automatically lost when you hit the floor. Your arms and legs need to move in circles and loops. No straight side-to-side linear stuff. By moving in loops you make up for more of the lost speed.

One of the things that truly determines the defen-

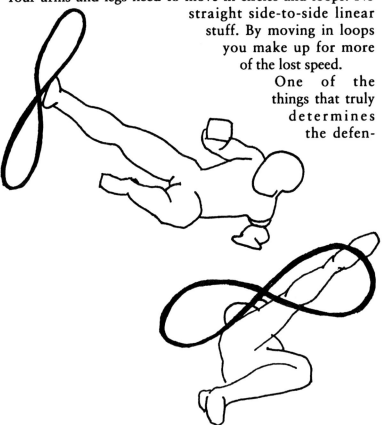

sive range is you can use your forearms, hands, lower legs, and feet as striking surfaces. You can stick them way the hell out there to stir up the pot. As long as you snake them out and back quickly, you're relatively safe from the chance of them being broken. Normally all you have to do is get enough out there to screw up his attack, which is, believe it or not, a whole lot less than most people think. It is going to be a rare cookie who is going to commit his entire body weight to a kick. If he did, he'd fall over. Like cooking, a proper strike mostly consists of getting everything to the table at the same time. Different processes are faster/slower than others. Most moves consist of getting three or four different sets of physics to converge at one point simultaneously. All you really need to do is screw up one of those processes.

For example, say you are kicking a soccer ball. What's going to happen is you shift your weight to one leg. This frees up your other leg to start the swing needed for the kick. It is the swinging of the leg and possibly the snap of the knee at the end of the swing that will send the ball flying. A leg is a heavy hunk of meat; in combination with a snap it can carry some serious momentum. Unlike walking forward, the body weight isn't entirely transferred to the forward foot during the kick. Most people kick a ball and, consequentially, a person on the ground like this.

In order to counter this action effectively, you don't need to move the person's entire body weight. Like I said, you screw up one part of this process and you essentially bring the whole thing to a complete halt. Nine times out of ten, the absolute most you'd have to do is deflect the weight of the person's leg in order to be safe. This means you don't need a block that is designed to try to take the impact of someone's entire body weight. The most you need to do is hit hard enough to F.U.B.A.R. his leg swing.[4]

Now, that leg swing is going to be moving slower than his knee snap. In fact, unless the guy has got boots on, which will basically turn the knee snap into a smaller leg swing, that snap will be too fast for you to be able to counter from the floor. That means you won't be fast enough to stop it once it gets moving. The combination of that pendulum of the leg and the snap arriving at the same time is beau coup dangerous. The good news, however, is your leg can move just as fast as his leg. In fact, with what you will learn in this chapter, your defense leg might be able to move faster since you don't have to pause to shift weight. This means you'll often be able to parry in time if you move your thinking up to the proper time zone. Observe the illustration below.

Let me point something out that is so basic that most

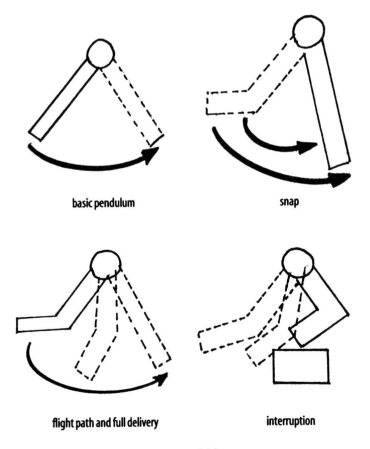

basic pendulum                    snap

flight path and full delivery          interruption

people don't really realize it. The knee only really bends one way. Because of this little fact, we are faced with a unique conclusion. Wherever the upper leg goes, the lower leg will follow. Face it: the knee determines the flight path of the lower leg. If you can spot the direction the knee is going, you know where the kick is going. On the ground it is nearly impossible to keep pace with the lower leg. The sucker is going too fast. However, it's not too hard to keep pace with the guy's knee. It's attached to his thigh, and that hunk of meat takes some time to move.

A truly effective fighter can deliver his body weight from any position that his move is interrupted in. Break out the champagne, folks, there aren't too many truly effective fighters. All you have to do is interfere with the guy's kick enough to either 1) deflect his knee or 2) prevent the snap from coming to completion. You either clip his leg hard enough to deflect his knee, or you stick something in the way before the snap can pick up speed. You know which route it's going to be taking. There's the knee; the snap can't be far behind. Now just stick something in there before the snap can start.

Here's another freebie. Most people don't start the snap until after their leg has passed the lowest point of the swing's arc (6 o'clock if you're head is 12 o'clock). If they did, they'd hit the ground with the foot they intended to kick with. Try this: stand up and stick your leg out behind you and keep it straight. Now try to bring it around the clock to the front. Grounds out around 7 o'clock, doesn't it? This is why most people's legs are still cocked when their thigh and knee are at 6 o'clock. All you need to do to screw up the process is have your leg in the flight path at 6 o'clock at the same time. Don't worry—that lower leg will be along shortly.

What this does is screw up the physics of his balance. If the guy was relying on his leg to be there to take his weight after he kicked you (as in a short hip kick or stomp), he's got some problems. Another potential problem is if you hit him from an angle on his leg, it might be enough to knock him over. Hell, he's only standing on one leg and moving at that. Know too many people who can take impacts while standing on one leg? I don't. This will make more sense when I talk about the triangle later on.

## THE "BEST" FLOOR FIGHTING POSITION

There really isn't a good place from which to fight from the floor. What you can get, however, is the least fucked-up position. If you can't get into this position, you better roll the hell out of there or crab it under a table lickety-split. I'm not joking about you tumble weeding it out of there. If you can't get up, out of range, or into this position against someone who is still standing, you might as well just kiss your ass goodbye.

The photos at right are your basic floor fighting position. It ain't much, but it's all you've got. The good news about this position is it regains as much as possible those elements you lost when you hit the floor. Furthermore, it is also deceptive and will often lure someone into your offensive range. While this may be the premier floor fighting position, I have to seriously warn you that it in no way overcomes the limitations of being on the floor against a standing opponent. He's still going to be faster and more mobile than you are. If the guy knows what he's doing, he'll slip it and take you out from the side. Or he'll pick up a chair and instead of bashing down overhand, do a golf swing with it. Not good, not good!

Often what will happen when you drop into this position is a trained fighter will slam on his brakes immediately. He won't make the mistake of an amateur and rush this stance from the wrong angle. He will try to slip around, and you need to spin with him. This is where it gets interesting . . . if you consider a mongoose and cobra hashing it out interesting. If he hesitates, use this time to chuck a chair at him to distract him long enough for you to spring up. I know a guy who was Green Beret in Nam who

was studying taekwon do in Korea. He got blown off his feet by the master. The master closed the distance to press his advantage. He nearly got his chest caved in for his trouble when my friend landed in this position and countered with a side thrust kick. The master backpedalled in shock that this American should know floor work. My friend utilized the time and got his ass back up.

An untrained fighter, or in the case of the taekwon do master, someone not expecting someone to know floor work, will often try to

*Front and side views of floor fighting position.*

113

*Proper position and distance.*

close the distance on someone in this position. This is good. When they do that, they enter into offensive range (evil chuckle). From there, you have a host of nasty counterattacks lined up to surprise them with.

Let's look at why this position is effective. Remember how I outlined the nine dangers of being on the floor earlier in this chapter? Let's look at them one at a time against this position.

1) Loss of mobility is the major danger to someone on the floor. This position is designed to allow you to be able to spin in whatever direction an attacker might position himself. While it has other purposes, the bottom leg primarily is used to propel you around in a circle to get your legs in place to meet any attack. The bottom arm also helps in this endeavor, as well as adding stability.

In cases like this, your pivot point becomes someplace

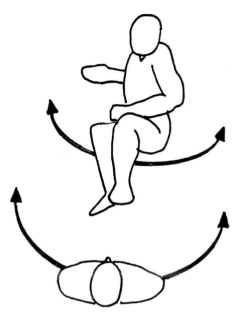

Floor pivot.

near the bottom of your rib cage. You spin around that point propelled by arm and leg. If your opponent tries to slip to the side, you scoot around so he is again facing your legs. The best way to attack someone on the ground is from the side; what this position allows you to do is make sure he never gets a chance to get to your side.

2) Your ability to move quickly is reduced. While this is still true, this position gives you some back. While it is not blindingly fast, you can propel yourself straight back by straightening your bottom leg. With practice you can literally swim backward by straightening one leg and, as you're scooting back, roll over to your other hip. That leg is cocked already. As you are straightening that one out, cock the first leg back again.

While this is not effective for long-distance travel, it often works for one or two scoots to buy you the time you need. By that time, the guy will have caught on to what all that flopping is about. A guy on his feet is still going to be faster than you are. On the other hand, you'd be amazed at how fast I've gotten under tables using this move.

While I've seen people recommend rolling on your stomach doing this move, I personally like my huevos too

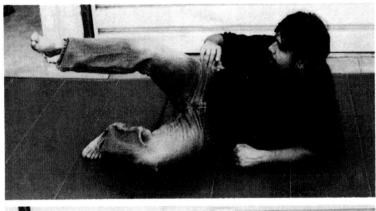

*Swim step.*

much to leave them exposed like that when I'm moving. I prefer to keep my knees up in the air and able to protect me against the unexpected during the process. With the stomach down, your legs are tied up on the ground. Yes time and energy is lost by doing it on my back, but I get to keep the family jewels. Your choice, of course.

The next joy about this position when held up to problem number two is your lower limbs are already curled up for an emergency bug out. If you are flat on your back, you definitely will lose time while trying to roll to the left or right. If your need for speed involves a swung chair, that's some seriously bad news. What this position does to compensate is to allow you to throw yourself one way or the other and add in any muscle you can muster from your bottom limbs. While the direction you'll be going is still either left or right, you'll be able to do it faster than expected.

Also, I should point out that most people don't expect you to be quick enough to roll away from an attack while on the floor. It usually comes as a surprise to them that their move didn't work. While they're standing there in shock, you're bouncing back to your feet. Every now and then you'll encounter a rocket scientist who watches too much TV wrestling. I've seen people literally throw themselves down onto someone on the floor. When you see him jump, roll out of the way and let him imitate a cow flop hitting the floor.

3) Reduced speed. Face it: you're on the ground, you've lost speed. However, this position frees your upper leg to defend yourself. How fast you are depends on how strong your leg muscles are. Another compensating factor is that your limbs are already positioned to strike. By the time the guy gets in range, you're ready for him. If you fell outside of defense range, he's got some ground to cover before he can be a threat to you. If you fell inside offensive range, you can convince him either to join you on the ground or that it's in his best interest to get the hell out of there.

4 & 5) On your back and all four limbs to defend vs. on

your side and limited bottom limb use. The problems about being on your back are pretty self-evident at this time. While it is true that being on your side limits the use of your bottom limbs as a defense, their new assignments of mover and stabilizer more than pay the cost. Also, as previously mentioned, that bottom leg is cocked in a floor fighting position. If you leave it straight out, it's useless not only as a mode of transportation but as a possible offensive factor as well. A cocked leg can be used, as you will soon see.

6) Only one direction is good for defense. Yep, that's true. The direction is from your feet. In case you haven't noticed it, this position is designed to scoot you around so your attacker has to come through that very direction.

7) Attacks from chairs and tables. What you have going for you here is that most people do not know how to attack effectively. If someone picks something up and either throws it at you or tries to swat you, it's usually going to come from one angle. That's the overhand, straight-down

swing. Remember, people don't have much experience floor fighting; even a streetfighter is going to get confused when faced with this position. Most brawlers are accustomed to kicking their downed opponents in the ribs and head. This is the extent of their repertoire. When confronted with someone who assumes the floor position, they're sort of at a loss. If the guy decides to use a tool, the odds are he's going to try the overhand swat. Remember, this is probably new territory for him, and most people aren't that creative in a new turf.

The real bitch is that if the guy does have experience, he's not going to try to swat you along the line that you're body is lying. Either he is going to sweep the chair across your legs or he's going to slip and try to strike down a line that is diagonal to your body. If he gets into that position, there's little you can effectively do to save yourself. You might try and kick to deflect the chair, but it's not even close to a guaranteed move.

8) Stomping by a mob from multiple directions. Well, you can't have everything. You may be able to deflect some with your arms and legs, but if you go down in a mob, you're in a heap o' trouble, boy. All I can recommend in this situation is look for a hole and try and get through it. This especially means scrambling under tables and other furniture. Around support poles is another good one to remember, as well as under cars. If it is a particular group with members, another slim possibility is if you can get one of them down with you. Grab onto him for dear life. Hopefully they'll be less likely to kick when one of their friends is down there. In a honky tonk bar, though, that may not work. Some places are just as likely to kick two people on the ground as one.

9) The dangers of committed weight while getting up. While I will deal with getting back up in another chapter, what this position does is, by curling your limbs, give you extra spring to bounce back up.

## THE "TRIANGLE" DEFENSE

Now that you've seen why this is the best floor fighting position around, we'll get into some of its applications. Since it has always been my contention that it is more important to be able to defend than it is attack, I'll start there.

The crux of your floor defense should be based in a triangle. I've explained why you don't want to take the impact of a blow when you are on the ground. Now I want to give you an idea that you should model your defenses around. Look at the illustration below.

Which one of those shapes is going to take the entire impact of the incoming blow? (Hint: It's not the one with three sides.) Whenever you interrupt an attack (like messing up a kick by knowing where the knee is going), what you want to do is deflect the energy down either side of the triangle. It makes more sense if you look at the illustration at the top of page 122.

While that is a simplified concept, it gets the idea across. Any energy that comes at you is met with this triangle. It moves around and meets any force from any direction. The pos-

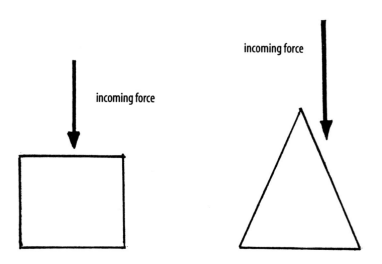

incoming force

incoming force

incoming force

triangle of defense

sibilities are illustrated at right.

When you practice with your friends, try to imagine this triangle moving to meet the oncoming attack. It's really easier to defend yourself if you learn to look at attacks in terms of angles and lines. No matter what kind of attack it is, it will come in on a certain line. By deflecting the line of attack away from you, you defend yourself effectively. Once you get the hang of thinking this way, you begin to instinctively know which way you need to angle the attack away from you to be safe.

Something I hear a lot when I teach this position is, "It leaves my nuts open!" Not really, but boy does it give you incentive to block! First off, your upper leg is there doing the triangle. That's line one defense. Secondly, there is your bottom leg, which with a quick twist of your hips and leg can save the day. A block with that leg will hurt like hell, but it is also a near horizontal block against a vertical attack. The odds are that horizontal and vertical will meet.

Also, from a psychological factor, your attacker will see an opportunity to kick you in the nuts. If he's so busy trying to do that, he often won't realize that he is trying to hammer through your strongest line of defense. It's the guy who immediately disregards your balls as a target and tries to go for your short ribs that you really have to worry about. Face it, unless you're Magilla Gorilla, his legs are stronger than your arms. You don't want to try to deflect kicks with your arms.

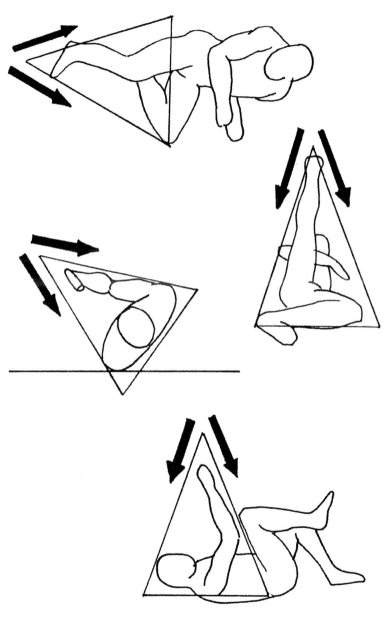

Defensive triangles.

It is preferable to keep your attacker out in defensive range. This is done by both scooting around and an occasional fast kick when he gets too close. Few people are good at throwing low long-distance kicks. That means he's going to be dancing around outside your range and not able to do too much damage until you get a chance to get back up. Sometimes, however, it will start tight and stay ugly as long as your attacker is still standing and in range.

A common close range attack toward someone on the floor is the stomp. I like stompers almost as much as I like people who walk up and flash a knife to impress me. As the flashy knifer has just given me the knife, the stomper has just joined me on the floor.

Let's look at the more impressive result of stomping first. Say it's a bad day in Bedrock. Somehow, in spite of all your efforts, the guy has managed to stay to your side. As he raises his leg to stomp, it looks like you're in a heap of shit. Not really. It is times like this that the triangle and roll are going to be a real surprise to ol' numb nuts. I hope he's limber, because if you got the room, he's going to be doing the splits real soon.

A stomp takes a person and puts him on one leg. A one-legged man in an ass-kicking contest is an old joke. Either you can simply roll into his support leg like a bowling ball or you can triangle and roll for more spectacular results. The basic roll is your body weight slamming into his leg and your arms tangling up his legs to keep him from regaining his balance. Most important is grabbing his stomping leg not only to prevent the stomp but to prevent him from stepping back with it to regain his balance. So long, Mom, I'm off to drop the bomb! This works better against a stomp that is aimed at your side that is closer to him.

Also, this move works against the short, brutal hip kicks that people will try to kick your ribs in with, although here you're going to have to take the kick and then grab his legs. It'll hurt, but the pay off is dropping him to the ground. You can still fight with a broken rib; multiple broken ribs or a rib

*Stopping a stomp I.*

driven through your lung makes it rough to keep going.

A more impressive and definitely more damaging version is a combination of the triangle and a roll. This works best if the guy is up near your torso, but if you're a real fancy dan, it can also be done with a foot hook. While it is a tighter move, you insert the triangle between his legs. This deflects the energy of the stomp away from you. This only works if the guy is stomping at your centerline or beyond, that is, the other side of your body, the side away from his leg. This happens—remember, in real fights people get sloppy.

What happens here is that your triangle deflects his stomp outward. If he were going to be able to complete this move, he would end up straddling you. Unfortunately for him, once you deflect the stomp to the outside you latch onto it in a death grip. You can do this by holding it with your hands or by tucking it into either of your armpits. If

*Stopping a stomp II.*

possible, you should try to jam your other arm into the back of his knee, as that will widen the circle and make this move more effective.

*Roll 'em, boys!* It's your body weight that makes this move work, not your grip on the back of his knee or on his leg. Once you have a hold of his leg, start rolling away from that guy with as much speed as you can possibly muster. There is both an offensive and defensive reason for getting the hell out of there quickly. Offensively, if you do it fast enough you'll drag the guy down into the splits. In case you don't know, most people can't do the splits. If they fall in this position, they'll tear ligaments and muscles. A torn leg muscle ends the fight real quick in your favor.

On the defensive front, if you're not fast enough the guy can bunny hop with you. He's going to do that long enough to realize that he can land on you with his knee. Also, if

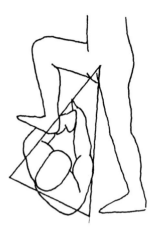

This sort of fall rips all
sorts of tendons.

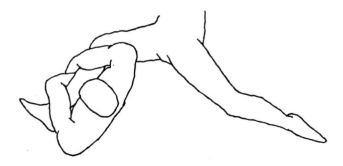

127

you're not fast enough you might just drag his knee down on you anyway. While this sounds risky, you being on the floor is more dangerous.

Often what will happen if you manage to drop into the floor position is your attacker will get frustrated with trying to kick you. When this happens, the guy will often try to shift over to stomping those pesky legs of yours. In case you haven't caught on, a stomp is a close-range move. Close-range moves mean that he's moving into offensive range. Either you can blow his support leg out from under him or, when he lifts his leg, hook him with your foot and jerk toward you. He's only on one leg and you're pulling the other. Guess what that means?

In order for this to work, you cannot allow him to regain control of his foot until he's past the point of no return. Believe me, as he realizes he's falling over, he's going to be battling to get that foot free. Your hook has to ride with him and keep him stretched out so he can't regain his footing. Once he's past the point of no return, you let him have his foot back. In fact if you're a real bright boy, while he's busy falling, you'll be taking this opportunity to get back on your feet.

What can go wrong with this move is the guy breaks away from your hook too early and regains his stability. Often this is accompanied by a step to regain stability, which changes his position, hence his angle. Or, if the guy is a superdick, he can leap with the direction of your pull. That's rarer than hen's teeth, but it is possible, especially if you're fighting someone who's trained in a South Pacific style. If he does that he's going to land in a place where he can kick you in the short ribs. Counter his counter with a pivot and again you're back to point A. By the way, an important safety tip for this move is get your other leg out of the way of where he's going to fall.

## OFFENSIVE GROUND TECHNIQUES

We've begun to move over into the realm of offense now. While the defensive range is mostly to keep the guy from closing with you, the offensive range is what you do when the guy has closed. If the guy is good, his attack will coincide with his closing. At times like this, you have to be more concerned about defending than attacking. This is the case of the guy who kicks in such a way that the three processes all arrive at the same time. He's putting his entire weight behind the move. The good news is that many people don't quite have their timing down. Often what will happen is the person closes first, then attacks. Of course we're only talking about a second's difference here, but if you've practiced, that is enough time. Another common thing is the guy closes and attacks at the same time, but when you foil his attack there is a moment's pause while he's regathering his forces. These are the two times to go on the offensive. You don't want to go on the offensive during the middle of his attack. While you can do "the best defense is a good offense" routine when you're on your feet, don't risk it when you're on the floor.

A good fighter will chain his attacks together. An excellent fighter will be like a rope wherein his attacks are points on the rope. Even with chained attacks there is usually a pause or a set-up period between attacks. You need to learn how to watch for these breaks in the movement. Someone who is throwing a punch will chamber back for a second punch. This is the break in attack that I'm talking about. Be warned that an excellent fighter will, by twisting, not break his flow of attack. While his arm is chambering back, he's using the same energy to throw an attack from the other side. This guy will not let you have time to counterattack. Against this sort of individual, you can only run, or in this case crab, away. This is someone who moves so fast and smoothly there is no perceptible break between attacks.

As I've pointed out, good fighters are rare, so most of what you're going to encounter is someone who has a break in his attacks. This is especially true with kicking. As you know, people are left- or right-handed. However, even most experienced martial artists are right- or left-legged. This means that most people kick more often with one particular leg. They put all their weight on one leg and kick with the other. This not only causes definite breaks between attacks, but it leaves them a sitting duck for certain counterattacks.

Basically, your normal human being is a triangle. (If someone isn't, I don't want to meet that person.) This triangle consists of two feet and a head, as shown in the illustration below.

You will notice that the person with his feet spread apart is a wider triangle than the one with his feet closer together. You might as well kiss off the idea of knocking the wider triangle over from the side. Sweeps, kicks, and scissor moves against this are a waste of time because the person's

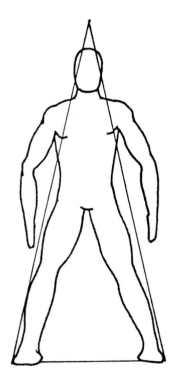

weight is equally distributed over a wide area. If you knock a foot out from under him, he's got lots of time to reposition it before he hits the point of no return.

While it is easier to take someone out in the narrower triangle, it is still no walk in the park. Up high, it's pretty easy—just apply enough pressure near the top fast enough that the person doesn't have a chance to widen his stance before he hits the point of no return. Unfortunately, you're on the ground working with the base of the triangle. First of all, you have to hit the base hard enough to overcome the person's weight bearing down. Rough to do with a kick. Secondly, you have to either hit so fast that the person doesn't have a chance to reposition his foot or get both feet over there so you can

trap the feet together. If you can do this, I'll give you a cigar. More often, you can finish this sentence regarding this move's success rate: "A snowball's chance in _____ ."

However, a person in the middle of a kick is a totally different situation. Look at the triangle at left.

Baby cakes, you now have an option. With that one foot down, he's got all his weight on one point. A one-point stance is not a strong one, especially against an attack to that point. A straight kick to the ankle does two things. One, it hits the only point of stability. Two, it hits directly equilaterally to what the person's stance integrity would be if he had two feet on the ground. In order for the guy to save himself, he has to get his foot near where his kick was

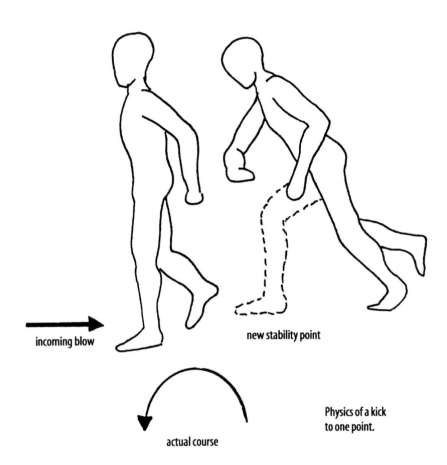

incoming blow

new stability point

actual course

Physics of a kick
to one point.

going before he hits the point of no return. No mean feat if he was in the process of chambering back for a kick.

With the sudden blowing out of his leg, his support is gone. His body is falling forward while his legs are out in the back forty. In order to save himself, he has to get a leg not under him but in front of him. He has to get his foot not to just 6 o'clock but actually what would have been his old position's 7 o'clock. He still has to get over the 6

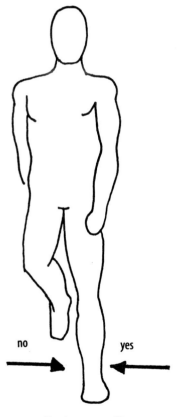

o'clock drag that I mentioned earlier. Furthermore, he has to get his new point of stability directly under his body to counteract the direction of his fall. Therefore, the actual course he'd need to take is the arc shown; otherwise his foot will drag out on the ground and not get there in time. The long and short of this equation is the guy would have to be awfully fast to keep from hitting the deck at this point.

The other way to mess someone's day up is with a round kick to the outside of his support ankle. If you hit him on the inside, all he has to do is bring his other foot down to regain stability. Any serious impact to the outside will start the process of him going over. In order to save himself he needs to do a mighty fancy cross step. You have to put your hip and leg weight into this move. This is not a snap kick—it's a full-blown bulldozer kick.

It has been my experience that kicks to the stability point are more effective than 95 percent of those fancy scissor moves. You have physics on your side in the form of the cocked leg giving your kick extra force to blow his leg out, but you also have the person's own stance integrity and stability working against him. Often what will happen is the schmuck will come in with a kick to your legs. This keeps him out in your defensive range and, consequently, out of his effective attacking

no                     yes

Blowing out an ankle.

range. When he does try to close through your defensive
range for a body attack, he puts himself in your offensive
range. The offensive range is an area where you can put
into your kicks as much of your body weight as the position
allows. If you try to reach out with a kick into your
defensive range, you can't get as much leverage in your
kick. The further out you go, the more energy you lose. In
your defenses, this doesn't mean anything, but in order to
take the guy down, you need enough energy and weight to
overcome his stability.

Another big advantage that you have is people don't
watch their ankles. They expect you to try for their knees or
groin. A low attack catches most people off guard. Unless
the guy is accustomed to speed hopping from foot to foot,
you're probably going to take him out with this move. Since
all of his weight is committed to that foot, it is easy to
break someone's ankle if you hit hard enough with a low
kick. Good news, that. The straight shots over the top of
the foot work best for this. Also, with this kind of kick,
make sure you hit near the heel of your foot. There is less
energy loss through the ankle if you hit with the heel,
whereas with the ball of the foot the ankle will flex. In fact
if you hit too hard with the ball of your foot, you might
break your own ankle.

## SPECIAL SITUATIONS

Earlier I said that there is a special situation where you
might want to block. Now that I've mentioned all the
components, I'll tell you under what circumstances. This
working to perfection depends on how tight your attacker
has got his shit wired. Against a sloppy joe it's really
effective, but it probably won't work against someone who
either is kicking correctly or wearing heavy boots. In truth,
this is less of a block than it is a collision. What I'm talking
about is kicking head-on into his kick. Instead of doing a
straight blast into his support ankle, you fire the kick down
the same tracks that his foot is coming in on. Remember,

the knee determines where the foot is going, and the flight path has to be altered to avoid the ground. With this in mind and a little bit of practice, you can usually predict where his foot is going to be coming from. Like old Casey Jones, you send your train down the same tracks for an appointment with destiny.

A premature impact often takes people unprepared. Put in simple terms, you can break the guy's foot if he isn't kicking correctly. This works better if you have hard shoes or boots on. If the guy himself is wearing soft shoes, this really increases the odds of his breaking something. I gotta tell you, you don't want to do this if he's wearing hard shoes and you're wearing soft ones. It would be bad.

This move is one of those wild cards. You can break someone's foot without them falling down (I know this from personal experience). While he may not fall down, a broken foot or toe will certainly slow him down. The odds are evened up for your escape. Who's faster—a guy skittling along on the floor or a guy limping along with a broken foot? On the other hand, even if you don't manage to break or sprain something, you might blow him off balance enough to bring him to the floor.

While I'm talking about exceptions that I mentioned earlier, I want to throw in the only time you want to be flat on your back. I've seen this happen not only in wrestling situations but when, against all rhyme or reason, someone who is standing throws himself onto a person on the floor. Like a lemming hurling himself off a cliff, they've thrown themselves onto a downed opponent. In either situation, or if you're both going down and he tries to land on top of you, try to get both legs up and under him, preferably in the abdomen area. What this does is curl you up. While being too tightly curled is not good (because you can't get enough leverage to do what I'm going to show you), you have to be tight enough to get your entire body into the spring.

Plant both feet on either side of his body and, with a snap, straighten your body out in a 45-degree angle off the ground. The feet must be placed so he can't spin off the thrust, which is what happens if you try this with only one foot. I have seen a 150-pound woman throw a 230-pound guy over 7 feet with this move. He would have gone much further, but a wall interrupted his flight plan. While this is normally a wrestling move, I bring it up here because of the possibility of the lemming hiking club.

Okay folks, let's talk about those special moves that the opportunity to use them only comes up every other leap year. Mostly I'm talking about scissor sweeps and takedowns. But there are many others that are floating around the hallowed halls of martial artdumb. You've now got most everything you need to evaluate them as seriously applicable vs. the "if the wind is from the northeast on an alternate Thursday" school of self-defense.

As I've mentioned . . . no let's change that . . . harped on again and again, there is an offensive range and defensive range of floor fighting. It is especially true with scissor sweeps that the guy has to be in offensive range. He has to be close enough for you to pin him with your thighs.[5] If you try to do it way the hell out there, he's not going over. Furthermore, you're left with your legs sticking way out there where he can start stomping them at his leisure. In case you don't know, it's hard to break a leg with an arm strike, but his legs definitely have enough juice to break yours.

Not only that, but your sweep's energy has to be perfectly equilateral against his stance integrity. The actual mover and shaker of a scissor sweep is in the roll, not the legs. Once you lock his legs up, you roll out of there. To further the problem, you have to be able, with the scissoring action of your legs, to prevent him from either simply stepping forward or lifting his foot out and setting it forward. In case you haven't noticed, most people's leg muscles aren't that strong on a forward scissor action. While many people can muster some serious strength in a side clam (thighs together), doing a swimming scissor with any strength is rough.

*Ineffective and effective ranges of floor sweeps.*

Let's add more to the stew here. Law number four is get up immediately. While the guy may fall toward you with a kick to his support leg, there still exists the chance that you can roll out of the way as he goes "Timber!" Now if you take him down in a scissor sweep, how are you going to get away with him all tangled up in your legs?

While I'm on a roll here, I want to point out one more thing that bothers me about scissor sweeps. The advantage of the floor position is that it gives you two lines of protection for your old testes. What does extending both of your legs out on either side of his stance leave you wide open for? Brrrrr!

● ● ● ● ● ● ●

What I have tried to do with this chapter is give you all the basic systems of staying in good health against someone who is still standing. You need to practice from two standpoints. Number one is seeing how these ideas work. Practice slow in this first phase. Stick your hand out there and experiment with some of the concepts I've explained. Once you have an idea of how they work, begin to speed up with your partner. This is two, the actual physical practice. While I may threaten your wallet later with a video on street wrestling, I've done what I could to get the basics across so you can practice them.

## FOOTNOTES

[1] That I tried to shift out of "street" by hanging out with a horde of functional psychotics amazes me to this day. Of course, there was always something about sharp blades and odd weapons that drew me that way. That's where I perfected the art of nonfirearm weapons fighting. Of course, living in Hollywood and other charming places allowed me to practice them regularly. Ever see what a battle axe can do to a car roof support? I have . . .

[2] ... whereas in the other story, because I fell in a certain way, I had some space and distance. There I was more concerned with buying even more distance in order to regroup my best defenses. Once he jumped away to avoid my chopping off his knee, I had enough space to get up safely.

[3] There is a special situation where you do want to be in this position, but we'll go into it in a bit.

[4] F.U.B.A.R.—World War II military acronym for Fucked Up Beyond All Repair.

[5] If you don't think that puts your nuts at serious risk, you're sadly mistaken.

# 5 WRASSLIN'

*"If you didn't see the fight start, and didn't see him actually bite the ear off, how in the blue blazes do you know that he bit the man's ear off?"*

*"I saw him spit it out."*

—From a court case

Okay, so you've invited company for your little floor party, smart man. Now that you got him there, whatcha gonna do? Once again, the answer goes against what most people think.

Come to think of it, let's take a look at that for a second. Amongst my other gonzo entertainments, I "boulder." This is rock climbing without ropes and pinions. It's also called free climbing. If you blow it while you're free climbing, that's it, you're screwed.[1] It was in rock climbing that I picked up a good term: "counterintuitive." That is any move which goes against your natural reaction. While it would seem that the most sensible thing to do 20 feet off the ground on a vertical surface is to hug the rock, that's not so. If you try to kiss the rock by getting your body close to the face, what you have just done is set up the perfect situation to lever yourself off the rock. To set up the proper physics to stay on a vertical face, you have to hang way off the rock and use your body weight as a counterweight that pushes your hands and feet *into* the rock. Instead of clinging close to what little earth you have around, you have to stick your ass way out into a whole lot of nothing. To say that action is "counterintuitive" is like saying Genghis Khan dabbled in real estate. In other words, the understatement of the century.

Many things I have mentioned in this book are counterintuitive until you get some experience. For instance, until you know what the "point of no return" feels like, you will more than likely continue vainly trying to regain your footing. Until they get that body knowledge, the idea of purposely throwing yourself out into the wild blue yonder will strike most people as a *"Are you out of your fucking mind!?"* proposition. This is exactly what counterintuitive movement is. Once you've been there, however, you begin to understand why the move makes sense.

Purposefully diving into a throw or roll is another counterintuitive move, as is charging a trap. Moving further into a locking grip sounds silly until you go out and practice it. I'm not the kind of guy who tells you to do something just because I said so. I spend a lot of time explaining the physics of a technique so you understand why I'm suggesting it. Since I'm doing this in a book, I can't show you how it works, I can only explain why it will work. While I once got accused of writing a "kinda technical" book,[2] I've found that people understand better if you give them an idea of the goal they're working for and why.

## DON'T PUNCH!

The reason I mention this counterintuitive issue is because it refers to a biggie, which I'm going to give you now. It's simple: "When you're on the ground, don't waste your time punching." Kinda goes against the grain, doesn't it?

I cannot begin to tell you how many times I've seen guys

rolling around on the floor trying to punch each other out. While some damage is done, it's usually more cosmetic than anything else. A normal trip to the floor results in messed-up hair and clothes and not much else. While the new hairdo may be a radical departure, it doesn't qualify as damage.

How many times have you seen guys rolling around the ground punching away at each other? Now, critical examination here, how much actual damage was done while they were rolling around? I'm betting very little. Most of the damage from punches would have been done when one guy got the upper hand and managed to rear up into a near sitting position. From there he can at least get his torso weight into his punches. Meanwhile, the guy on the bottom continues to throw inefficient punches from the ground.

While you can hook effectively from the floor, a full-scale out-and-out punch is a waste of time. You simply cannot get your body weight into it. All that you're doing is using the muscles in your arm to strike with. Shit, I can take arm-powered punches all day long. It's a punch backed with body weight that does the damage. Now I want you to try to figure out a way you can throw a punch while lying on the ground that gets your body weight involved. If you're alone (or you got understanding roommates), try lying on the floor and throwing a good punch.

If you came up with anything, I'm betting that it's a tight hook or a short uppercut. A powerful, fast, wide hook[3] is just not really possible from the floor. Face it, you're on the floor, the options are kind of limited in which way you can move. It is here that most people blow it with floor fighting. They try to continue with the same tactics that they use while on their feet.

## GROUND MAULING TECHNIQUES

So how do you damage someone while you're both on the floor? There are three basic ways to do this: 1) gouging techniques, 2) maiming techniques, and 3) short shots (jabs/uppercuts/head butts).

Number one is the fine art of placing your thumb in the guy's eye. Numbers two and three are related in that they both use the little body weight that you can muster in short, sharp movements. Number two is based on drawing away suddenly and taking a piece of him away with you. Number 3 usually is based on putting his respiratory system on the fritz, although there are a few nasty variations.

The idea of winning a street wrestling match has little to do with putting your opponent into some kind of hold and more to do with maiming him so badly that you can get up quicker than he can. Once you're back up, either you try to kick his ribs in or you beat feet out of there to avoid attack from his cronies.

Unlike normal wrestling, you're not going for the pin. See, there's something about human nature that, if people see their friend getting his ass kicked, they'll jump in. If you pin the guy, your body weight is pretty well committed to the pin, too. This means you're a sitting duck for any outside attack. You will notice that most throws result in one guy on the ground in a locked-out position while the thrower is still standing. If another attack comes, he can neutralize the guy on the ground (what a nice way to say break his arm) and turn to face the new threat. If you're tied up on the ground, however, you can't face a new threat effectively.

Now the good news about this situation is that most people—after they discover that punching isn't working—will try to go for a hold of some form. This gives you lots of time to maul them. While he's trying to grab, you're gouging. Often what will happen is when you get a knuckle dug in good and deep, the guy will try to break away. Use this action as your distance to get up. If the guy tried to grab you and got seriously maimed the first time, he's not too likely to try to grab you again. In fact, he's probably going to be more interested in getting the hell out of there than he is keeping you on the ground.

Locks on the ground are more joint breakers than they are holds. This puts them in the category of maiming techniques. I've snapped many a wrist and arm in the middle of a grapple. You break his joint and get out of there. He's not likely to follow you.

There is point that, while manifestations differ radically, the basic concept remains constant. That is the action of a short, sharp movement. Jerk, jab, gouge, twist—they all have this in common. Because your operating space is limited, your motions become smaller, tighter, and faster. You're not trying to run a marathon here; all of your actions have just shifted over to short dashes. On the ground, you have to move your weight in a space of mere inches rather than feet. Wrestling is the ultimate in-fighting technique, and you have to utilize your weight accordingly.

*Twisting and Arching*

I need you to lie down on the ground again. Lying on your side, put your arm out in front. Now, jerk your body back as far as it can go and still stay on your side. If you roll onto your back, you've gone too far. Do the same with a forward motion (as if you're punching someone who's lying next to you). These are the "backward" and "forward" twists. The next move is to put your elbow on your side so your forearm sticks out parallel with the floor. Now arch your back so the bottom of your rib cage sticks out and your head and feet are thrown back. This is the "forward arch." Reverse the process so the part of your back that your elbow is resting over sticks out the furthest. Your head and feet now are the furthest point going the other way. As you might have guessed, "backward arch."

Those four basic actions are the core of 90 percent of the moves that can be done in mauling categories two and three. The forward arch is for strikes. The back arch is for draws, maiming rips, and head butts. The forward twist is for jabs to the short ribs, while the back twist is for certain draws and rips. These are often combined with shoulder raises or drops for extra power. You'll notice that you can only move so far quickly while doing these moves. After

145

that, the drag of the floor interferes with your motion. Your effective range of movement is in the distance that you can move quickly. All of your strikes and maiming moves must operate in this area to be effective. Granted while you're practicing how to move down here you'll look like you're having an epileptic seizure, but in order to move well on the floor you must practice!

To be an effective wrassler (as opposed to a competition wrestler), you must be able to move your entire body weight quickly within that area of free motion. Most people mess up because they try to maneuver beyond that free-motion zone. Once you get outside that zone, you lose energy and speed. Therefore the move must stop before you go out of the zone in order for all the energy to be delivered. Another factor to consider is that the type of floor you're on will affect how far you can move. Rugs will add drag (and rug burn) to your maneuver more so than a linoleum floor.

Let's put this into practical application. Using the forward arch—that's where, with your elbow on your hip you arch your back forward so your ribs stick out—practice moving to the limit of the free-motion zone. It's important that you stop before you move out of the zone. Once you can do that quickly, add in a shoulder rise. That means as your body reaches the stopping point, your shoulder reaches up as far as it can go at the same time. It's a weird jerk that doesn't make much sense until you add in the uppercut. Your elbow is still tucked against the side of your body—it's not swinging side to side, it's locked against your body.

The action of the forward arch in combination with the shoulder rise gives you an effective uppercut to his diaphragm. If you've ever had "the wind knocked out of you," you know what he's going to be going through. An uppercut to the diaphragm not only causes temporary paralysis of the diaphragm, but it knocks out all of the air pockets that normally stay in the lungs. Without these air pockets he would feel as if he were suffocating between breaths.

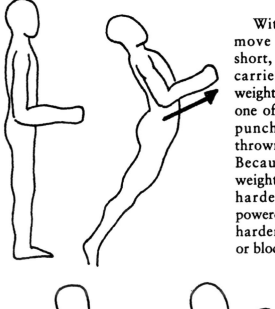

With practice, that move will deliver a short, sharp blow that carries as much body weight as possible. It is one of the few effective punches that can be thrown on the ground. Because of the body weight involved, it hits harder than an arm-powered punch, and it's harder to knock away or block.

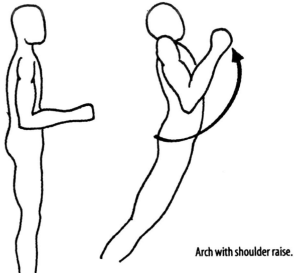

Arch with shoulder raise.

The next most important thing to realize is that while you can fire away with a few wild punches when standing, on the ground targeting is everything. An uppercut to his chest may bruise muscles, but it's not going to stop him. A blow to his diaphragm will do most of the work for you.

147

As we proceed, I'll cover the best and worst targets. You just have to realize here that the shit seriously tightens up on the ground.

### Gouging Techniques

We're first going to look at the area of "gouging." The term not only includes trying to roto-till your thumb into the guy's eye, but it also includes trying to move his nose to the other side of his head.

Although the head really is not that good of a target for a punch, with gouging techniques: "PARTY, PARTY, PARTY!" There are five key target areas on the head that are susceptible to attack. They are the eyes, nose, mouth, ears, and back of the jaw.

There are a few ways to go for a guy's eyes. Oddly enough, while sticking your thumb directly into a guy's eye hurts, it's not that effective. The better (and more painful) way is from around the edge, especially the inside near the nose.

Basically, the eye is a ball sitting in a cavity or socket. Any direct pressure will simply compress the eye back into the socket. Painful, but not nearly as ugly as from the side. See, a gouging action from the side allows the eye to try to slip out the side.

Another little thing that makes the side gouge more painful is the same thing that makes getting your scrotum yanked so painful. See that "Y" shape behind the eye? That's the optic nerve. As your testicles are connected and can only

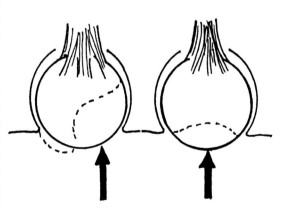

yo-yo out so far before they become extremely painful, so is the eye connected. A side gouge makes it more likely to put strain on that tethering nerve.

There are a few ways to go about an eye gouge. They can come either from the front or the back. Now, how seriously you want to damage the guy determines how badly you dig in. If he's trying to stick a knife in you, popping his eye out of his head is probably justified. If, on the other hand, it's just a scuffle at a party, slicing his eyeball open with your fingernail is too extreme. You can quickly slip onto the wrong side of a reputation if you don't learn how to exercise control over your fighting. Also, if you gouge someone's eye out unjustly, his friends will come looking for you. A shotgun blast or a few rounds from a 9mm into your car at a stoplight is sort of hard to dodge. Of course, it's always open season on muggers and rapists.

The thumb punch, where your thumb is supported by your forefinger, is for direct forward pressure. The thumb sticking out to the side is for sideward motions to dig in. In either case, your thumb is an auger backed up by your fist. A common trick of old-time kali fighters (I mean the real ones, the guys who came out of the slums and barrios, where it isn't a martial art, it's survival) is sharpened fingernails like you see in the photo.[5] It is definitely an eye slicer. Unless you live in an area where the weekend body count does not even make it to the news, I wouldn't recommend getting this extreme.

What makes the thumb punch effective is it is a straight-on attack. On the ground it's hard to

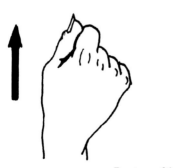

Two types of thumb gouge.

move quickly out of arm's reach. If you go in on the nose side, him twisting his head either digs your thumb in further or hangs it up on his nose. If someone throws any sort of eye gouge on you, get your arm up there immediately and block. Knock it up onto your forehead and come in with your own gouge.

*Lever eye gouge.*

Another good gouge is the lever. Your fingers are placed against his temple and your hand arched. Using your fingers as a pivot point, you lever your thumb into his eye. What really makes this effective is it gives you the closest thing to a grip that you can get with an eye gouge. If the guy tries to jerk away, you can follow him and keep the pressure on. What the hell, though; if he's backpedalling, let him go and use the space to get back up.

I learned the other good eye gouge technique from a guy who was doing it incorrectly on me. Afterward I sat down and figured out what he was doing wrong. It's when you reach around from behind and glom on to his eyes. What the guy was doing wrong was that he was trying to squish my eyes into my head rather than gouge them out. You're suppose to curl your hands into hooks and drive your fingertips into the eyes. The guy was pulling straight back rather than digging in with his fingertips. (Remember, if someone pulls a move on you in a fight, always analyze it later. If it worked, remember it. If it didn't work, analyze why and if the flaw can be corrected. If it can't be corrected, throw it onto the trash pile.)

You can pick your friends, and you can pick your nose, but you can't pick your friend's nose. Wanna bet? The next area of gouging is the old snot locker itself. Imagine the fun you'll have hooking your pinky up some guy's nose. It's loads of fun to watch him wiggle like a worm on a hook to get your finger out of his nostril. The action is upward toward his eyes or up and outward. A long little finger nail makes it all the more imperative for him to squirm away. Think a pinky won't make you move? Imagine having an Xacto blade shoved up your schnozzolah. You'll move.

For those of you who are more genteel in your gouging practices, there's always plastering his nose to the side of his face. Face it, the nose only has so much flex. Putting your palm against his nose and trying to shove it around to his ear sort of exceeds designer specs. The nose is supposed to stick out from the face, not lie flush with it. This move is not good for a long-term grip, as he can usually escape it with a snap of the head. However as a passing move to buy you time to prepare something really nasty, it's pretty good. It's also great for distracting him long enough for you to slip out of whatever particular nasty he's trying to lock you into. It works better

Nose hook.

*Nose sweep.*

the higher up the honker you apply it.

Probably the best move for breaking his concentration regarding his nose is the upward sweep. I've only met one person who managed to resist this move, and even then it was only a partial resistance. I was originally taught this as a one-finger move; applied research, however, says the best way to do it is to use the side of your hand. This consists of slapping your hand over his mouth so the side of your hand touches the base of his nose. Then you slide your hand upward toward his eyes. If you are using the thumb side of your hand, his nose slips into the V of your thumb and fingers. You then continue to lift.

While cartilage has the ability to bend, you will notice it usually bends in directions where it's not anchored down. The nose sweep goes exactly along the line that the cartilage is anchored. Long and short of that one, bucko, is it isn't going to flex too well. To the guy, it will feel like you're trying to drive his nose into his brain. If he's stupid enough to believe that fantasy about his own "nose bone" splitting his brain, he's really going to leap back.

While it is better to do this move with the thumb V, you can also do it with the pinky side of your hand. Unfortunately, this way does not have as much control as the other. Now, one thing people ask me about regarding this move is the likelihood of getting bit. Well if you leave your hand out there after he's shaken it off, hell yes you're going to get bit. On the other hand, as long as you have your hand flat against his face, the only way you can be bitten is if he gets his hand up there and shoves your hand in his mouth. Try it; hold your hand to your nose this way and try to bite your hand. Maybe if you have mandibles you can succeed. I was originally taught this move with my index finger under the nose, but that's too easy to escape from, although it is kind of fun with obnoxious people at parties.

We now move onto one of the most gouge-sensitive areas on the human body. That is the place below the ear and behind the jaw. I've tried to find a name for this area, but I haven't been able to find one. I do know that a direct gouge here by thumb, knuckle, or finger hurts like hell. The same thumb gouges that work for the eyes work here. In fact, those are the standard thumb-gouging positions. You have to dig straight in for the fireworks, but boy will you get results.

Evidently, there are muscles, glands, and a cluster of nerves behind the jaw that makes this area so vulnerable. As near as I can tell, as well as digging in between the stylohyoid and digastric muscles and separating them, one of the spinal nerves gets crunched when you go rooting around in there with your knuckle. All technical jargon aside, it fucking hurts to get gouged there. You can also snake in a phoenix punch into this area and get good results.

While it would seem like a good time to try to strangle your opponent while you're on the ground, I don't recommend this because it takes too long. There are faster ways to mess up someone's breathing, which I will go into later. On the other hand, you might encounter someone who doesn't share such an enlightened position. If someone tries to strangle you while you're on the ground, the escape action is basically the same if the guy is on top or to the side of you. Lace your arm from the outside in between his forearms, preferably so your arm goes over his lower arm and under his overhand arm.[6] From there, depending on how he's got you gripped, rotate your arm either clockwise or counterclockwise in front of you. It may help to use your other hand for extra push.

The other hand acts as a way to add extra force to the levering open of his grip. This is a more complicated way of escaping than simply snaking your arm over one of his arms and shoving it into your armpit. That technique, if you can use it, is better. However, if the guy is sitting on your chest, you may not be able to twist around enough to do it. It never hurts to know at least two ways out of every trap.

While a strangle move may not work, a knuckle gouge at

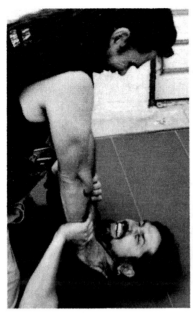

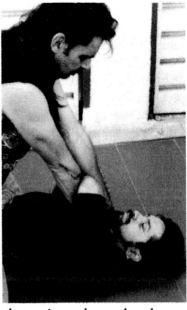

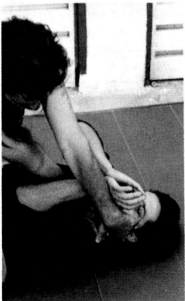

the point where the throat
intersects with the sternum
hurts like a mother and interferes with his breathing.
Another good area is under the
armpit into the rib cage. This
area is between the pectorals
(chest muscles) and the
latissimus dorsi (lats or wings).
Stick your knuckle in there
and shove. Hurts, don't it?

Moving further down the
torso, you get into the floating
ribs. While a gouge between
the ribs hurts anywhere, since
these aren't solidly connected
to the spine and sternum like
their uptown kin, the floating

*Breaking a stranglehold.*                    ribs are more susceptible to a

good gouge. I don't know why,
but the sides of the rib cage are
more tender to gouges than the
front. Oh, for these a phoenix fist
works best. You can get more
pressure than with your thumb.

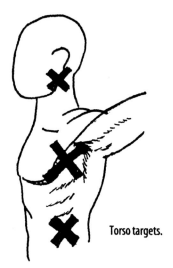
Torso targets.

This pretty much covers
gouges as such. While there are
other moves who's efficiency
can be improved in a gouging
action, they are basically jabs
and hooks. Some of the gouges
can be increased by turning
them into phoenix punch jabs.

### Maiming Techniques

Up to this point, the techniques I've discussed haven't
needed the jerking moves that I covered earlier. We're now
moving into that range. As I explain the moves, I'll tell you
which action—forward arch, backward arch, forward twist,
and backward twist—makes them most effective. Let's look
at maiming moves first.

There are three basic categories of grips that work with
maiming moves: the gorilla grip, martial arts claw grips
(eagle, tiger, dragon, etc.), and teeth. Yes, me buckos, I'm
talking about biting. This is not a dissertation on ballet; it's
about hurting someone before he hurts you. In combat you
use whatever you can, including biting parts off someone if
he leaves it sticking out there.

I should warn you that the human mouth is more septic
than a dog's mouth. There are reports of people dying from
infection from a human bite. Usually this has to do with the
person being bit not going to the hospital and the wound
festering. Of course if you bite off his ear, the odds are he's
going to go to the hospital. As long as you don't swallow it,
the doctor can usually sew it back on. The bad news about
biting someone who dies is that supposedly the person who

did it can be brought up on murder charges. While I don't maintain that biting is "for girls," I do recommend careful consideration before you start chewing on your opponent.[7]

You really don't want to get someone else's saliva in your blood. This is what is seriously wrong with punching someone in the mouth. All too often you'll cut your hand on his teeth and his saliva mixes with your blood. Bad news, that. Leads to infections right quick. I'm not sure how toxic saliva is to most germs, but if you get blood in your mouth, spit it out and wash out your mouth immediately.[8] While some people worry about various diseases they may catch by having someone's blood on them, I always worried more about explaining it to the cops. Being covered in blood is not conducive to convincing the cops that it wasn't you involved in that big brawl three blocks over.

Maiming grips work best on small appendages (yes that is an insult). Starting high again, the three most susceptible areas on the head are the nose, ears, and mouth. With all the fancy kung fu grips that abound, the best way to rip someone's nose out of its socket is to bite down and do a sudden back arch. Even if you don't manage to peel his nose off his face, the combination of the strongest muscles in the human body glomming on to his nose, then being torn free by your moving body weight, is going to hurt like hell.

When I was a kid I got in a fight with a kid named Billy something or other. He and I had not liked each other from the moment we laid eyes on each other. Finally it erupted into a knock-down drag-out in front of my house. With my first stepdad looking on, we tore into each other.

Billy kept on biting me. He got me on the thumb, arm, and back. This disturbed me, as I thought that was fighting dirty. (It shows you how long ago this was. I still had ideas on fighting fair.) Finally I said the hell with it and I chomped onto him square on the nose. It must have looked funny with me hanging onto his nose by my teeth. He broke away and we both went tumbling down to the ground.

When I landed, his left side was toward me. I wasn't finished playing jaws yet, so I latched onto him there. He was caterwauling and howling while throwing me around, but I was locked on like a leech. Finally he threw me off and took out of there.

I limped into the house, where my dad did the Bactine routine on my bites. Billy's mother called raising all sorts of Cain, and my stepdad calmly told her to go fuck herself. He'd seen the fight and knew who started biting. (Also, he was from East LA. We only got in trouble for fighting if we lost.) Next day, dear old Billy had beat me to school and shown everybody a softball-size black and blue bruise from where I had nailed him. Oddly enough, he didn't mention his nose. If he hadn't been such a shit, everyone would have probably believed him about my starting the fight. Oddly enough, nobody ever messed with me in that particular school again.

I sort of lost my reservations about fighting dirty after that little tête-à-tête. Even if you don't get an appendage, a good solid chomp onto the guy's body seriously messes him up. If the guy breaks free and boogies, let him go. If, on the other hand, you clamp on and he starts hitting and hurting you, let go and go after another form of attack. No need to soak up unnecessary punishment.

The next area that works as a target for maimers is the lips. While you can hook a thumb inside his cheek and pull to the side, you have to get out of there before he quits trying to resist and instead tries to bite your thumb off.

A number of those fancy kung fu maimer grabs work very well when you combine them with a forward arch. Grab ahold of his lower lip and try to rip it off. A gorilla grip combined with trying to pull his lip down to his navel will give a guy the closest example of what giving birth feels like that a man can experience. While you are not likely to get a ticker tape result, the stress and strain does smart. The motions of the arch are aided by a shoulder drop and downward arm jerk. Unlike a punch, everything starts at once rather than arrives at once. You're trying to hurt him as you pull away; therefore for all the energy to hit in the beginning, you have to put all the energy where you want to do the damage. The speed of the motion is supposed to overcome the elasticity and flex, while the muscle overrides the resistance that would slow you down.

Moving onto the ears. Take a look at the way your ears are connected to the side of your head. They are glued on in an up and down direction. That's how you want to try to take them off. While it would seem easier to pull forward, you can't get as good of a grip that way. There's a lump of cartilage that makes the ears stick out at an angle rather than lie straight back. Because of that lump, you can't get much more than a glorified pinch as a grip. Furthermore,

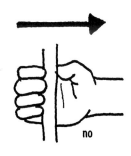

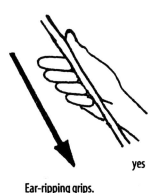

Ear-ripping grips.

the direction of this pull will take them right out of you hand's point of weakness. You encounter the same problem trying to pull them backward. Slippery little suckers.

What you have to do to maim someone in this manner is grip his ear along the line of your thumb and the ball of your thumb. Then you clamp down with all of your fingers, pinning the ear against the ball of your thumb. This locks it into your grip. Once you have that in place, you just lock your elbow and do a forward arch with a shoulder drop. This pulls the ear along its attachment direction (the direction in which it isn't flexible).

Until you get major practice on this (or you get damn

lucky), you're not likely to actually tear his ear off. You may tear it some, but it takes serious precision to snatch an ear off. To rip an earring out isn't so hard, however. The earlobe is flexible, and you can twist the earring around to get a good grip. Studs and pins are too hard to actually tear the ear, but danglies and hoops tear out nicely. Straight down or past his chest is the angle you want to go for.

If nature laid a pair of claws on you like a lobster, maybe you might want to try an eagle kung fu grip to the throat. While it's technically possible to rip someone's throat out, I've never seen it done in a bar fight. For the rest of us people with plain old hands, you can often reach up and dig in enough to make it hurt when you arch back.

Another area of maiming consists of digging your fingers behind muscles and jerking backward. While muscles can take an impact, jerking them away from the body hurts like hell. This action strains everything—tendons, nerves, veins, arteries. Everything is tethered down, so pulling strains the tethers. Unless you're Chop Saki, Master of the Martial Arts, you're probably not going to do permanent damage to the guy, but these hurt like a mother.⁹ Of these, the best known target is under the pectorals (chest muscles). You grab onto the guy's chest, dig your fingers in from the side (under the armpit), and arch backward.

If for some God awful reason you find yourself fighting with a woman, it also works on them. While I personally feel that there are many better ways to spend your time with women, I have had one attack me in the line of duty. We landed on a guy and she landed on me. Jesus! What do you do? This is why cops so hate "domestic" calls—instead of stopping the violence, it often turns on them. (For the record, I am rabidly against violence with your spouse or lover. Nonetheless, it doesn't hurt to know.)

Some people recommend driving your fingers under the rib cage. While I found that this hurts, I never found it to be debilitating. If you can figure out a way to do it to the diaphragm with a forward arch, more power to you.

Now let's look at one of the best targets for maimers, but one that is generally ignored. Put your iron claw on and reach for his nuts. Yeah, I know, most people have reservations about grabbing a guy's crotch. I'm not telling you to bite it, just crush it or rip it off.

Either a finger hook underneath the scrotum or a full on kung fu grip does the trick. In the case of the hook, a back arch with a shoulder lift will convince him to go away. Remember, they're like yo-yos—they can only travel so far before the line goes tight. With the kung fu grips, you have a few options. A back twist with the elbow locked to your side, a forward arch with a shoulder drop and driving your arm further between his legs, or a backward arch with a shoulder lift and a biceps curl all will have him singing like a birdy. Of course, just the old-fashioned gorilla grip crush will also get his attention.

I already discussed most other moves that could be considered maimers in the throws chapter. They are the various grips that I showed you how to break out of. Even without body weight, if you do them fast enough you can break wrists and arms. This is especially true with the thumb grab.

One that bears special mention, however, is the finger snap. You're not snapping your fingers, you're snapping his. Not much to it—grab onto his finger and twist your wrist suddenly as if you're rolling up the back of his arm.

While the action is simple, I would like to add some pointers. If you have to turn your wrist in an outward direction roll, you have to do it very quickly. This is because you have less area to move because your wrist only moves so far in that direction. If you do it slowly, he can compensate by bending his wrist back. While you can countercompensate by adding in an arm motion down his arm, it's getting sort of involved by now. Therefore if and when you start the move, add in a jerk down the back of his hand.

Another thing to consider is which finger to take out. While the index finger looks tempting as a target, the middle is the pièce de résistance. First off, he can't punch very well with a broken middle finger. Simple equation—it hurts him more than it hurts you. This limits his counterattacks immediately. For a long-term nasty, however, a broken finger means a cast. If they decide to just splint it instead, the middle finger is just as big of a problem as a cast. While you can work without the index finger, leverage against the palm is seriously reduced when the break is in the middle of the palm.

### Short Shots

On to short shots. I've already explained how to toss an uppercut into his diaphragm. An uppercut into his floating ribs is less effective but still gets results.

A hook is possible to the floating ribs, although it takes practice with the forward twist in order to deliver effectively. Again, this is something where you keep your elbow tucked tight against you and locked so your entire body weight is delivered. Although I've railed against the one-punch myth, I seriously have to tell you that on the floor you're not going to get the job done with only one punch. No knockouts from punches here, folks. The good news, however, is that both of these shots are designed to interrupt his respiratory system.

Now the ultimate respiratory system interrupter is the punch to the throat. Since you're on the floor, you're not likely to manage to get enough juice to collapse his windpipe. Yet if there is one place where you can get away with throwing a loop punch without body weight, this is it. A shot to the throat will stop damn near anyone. While the guy is panicking about not being able to breath, you can scurry away.

Let's look at the next great short shot, the head butt. Was there ever a more dastardly deed, a lower blow, a more despicable act? Gosh, I hope not. I'm sort of fond of the head butt. I'd hate to have to give the title to another move. This is a technique so frowned upon that serious Muay

Thai fighters aren't invited to play with the martial arts world until they drop it (and elbows) from their style (kickboxing is cleaned up Muay Thai). Next to the silat heel hook/sweep that drops your opponent into the splits, this is one of my favorite nasty in-fighting moves. On the wrestling circuit, such a move will get you banned for life.

Now some people say you should try to knock your opponent out with a head butt. I say there are easier things to do. I've tried to knock someone out with a head butt and what I managed to do was knock my ass just as silly as I did his. Instead of just one of us lying there grogged out, we both were. Fuck that noise!

Face it, if you're face-to-face with someone, the two most well-protected sections of your skulls are facing each other, too. Your forehead is an incredible feat of engineering; it can take some mighty big impacts. But here's the bad news: *so can his!* There're all kinds of theories as to how to do this move right. Unfortunately, not too many people are willing to volunteer to get KOed so a guy can practice. While I've heard all sorts of speculation as to how it's done, and I've seen guys smash bricks with their heads, I've never seen anyone effectively knocked out by a head butt. In my definition, effective means the guy who did it isn't looking at all the pretty birdies for awhile himself!

What I have seen (and done myself) is someone's *face* turned into guacamole with a head butt. I also have a deviated septum because of a backward head butt by a drug freak-out we landed on. (I snore like a buzzsaw because of it.) So one might say that I have some experience with this move.

The point of aiming at his face instead of his head is that the structure of the face is less fortified than that of the forehead. I can tell you there is nothing that will catch your attention faster than someone's forehead smashing into your face at a high speed. A new definition of pain is often discovered at moments like this.

While the head butt can be done by a snap of the neck, it get's real ugly when combined with a back arch. [1] While theoretically you tuck your chin into your chest to deliver maximum body weight, I always opted for more speed by adding in a forward neck snap. Generally this ended up with my chin against my chest anyway. I don't know what this does to the likelihood of you hurting yourself, but I guess it's sort of risky. I doubt that a chiropractor would be willing to tell you how to safely smash someone's facial bones into a gelatinous mass. (Any chiropractors out there? I'd love to know.) Anyway, keep your muscles tight when you do this move, as it shields the vertebrae and transfers energy better.

If you see someone rearing back to lay one of these babies on you, get the hell out of there! The back arch is kind of obvious when someone does it. If the guy is trying to get away, he'll be pushing you; if he's getting ready to puree your face, he'll grab onto you. You snap into a back arch so fast you look like a U-turn. Another thing to remember to do is gorilla grip him with a straight-arm lock-out. I'm talking arm's length here. That way when he dives forward, your arms transfer his body's energy to you and keep you away from him.

If you can't peel out of there in time, the next best thing to do is get your arm out in front of you—upper arm straight out and elbow aimed at the middle of his chest, then lock your arm. Usually, since you're lying down snuggling, you won't be able to get your arm straightened out, but that's okay. You want his chest to hit you straight on your elbow anyway. Your upper arm, being locked, will transfer the impact into your shoulder and body. You may have to angle up to compensate for the arc his body is traveling. If you're lucky, what will happen is the guy's own force will blow you out of his grip. If you're not so lucky, the least this will do is slow him down so you can get out of the way. Try not to hold your hand in line with your face, as you can end up hitting yourself when he runs into your arm.

Finally, the last-ditch "oh shit" measure is to tuck your chin down and meet him forehead to forehead. Never mind you're running the risk of brain damage, concussion, being knocked out, or dislocating your neck. So's he. As you can see, I don't recommend this defense until all else has failed. But instead of just you going to the hospital with a cracked skull, he goes too. Comforting this is not; practice the other two defenses until you're good at them.

Another bit of fun you can have with the backward arch is the knee to the groin. Here what you're doing is sticking the knee out and using your body snap to try and crush his nuts. There is very little actual leg movement, as it is too easy to lose impact when your legs are relaxed enough to move. This move requires serious practice of the sudden sharp snap into the back arch. Practice it by lying down next to your couch and kneeing it. I might recommend knee pads; after all, "the couch is mightier than the crotch."

If you are blessed with a heavy bag or a duffel bag that you can stuff with heavy soft stuff, lay it down and practice strikes and jerks. You can practice squirming around the floor all you want, but a few rounds with a strike surface will teach you more about the physics involved than all the wiggling in the world. In fact, duffel bags are inexpensive at surplus stores. Since all you're going to be doing is hitting it, you can get a cheap one. When it rips, duct tape the thing until it looks like a mummy silverfish.

Let's look at another aspect of wrestling. What do you do when it's not going your way? How do you get out of a situation where the guy is sitting on your chest and winding back to beat your head into the concrete? This is something you should wonder about.

The best way out of this picture is in a move called "the bridge." Basically, this move is one where you suddenly arch your body and send him flying off you. If you think this is something that you can do without practice, you are wrong. He will just put another quarter in your ear and wait for the ride to begin again.

What makes this move work is you put both feet flat on the ground with your knees pointing straight up. The actual lift comes from your legs, with additional help from arching your body. The motion will lift you off the ground so only your head/shoulders and feet are still touching.

Believe it or not, if the guy is sitting on your arms as well, this is better for you. That's because you can throw in a shove from your arms, too. If you have your arms free, use them to throw him off. The actual bridge works better if you twist one way or the other as you do it. Instead of two shoulders on the ground, you now have only one. What this does is fling him off in a direction other than toward your face. In order to do this technique right, everything has to be a simultaneous move. I have seen more people piggybacked around the floor by someone who couldn't get everything moving at once than I care to believe.

I heartily recommend you go out with your friends and practice this move on something soft. Unlike other moves, since the guy's body weight is on top of you, you really do have to get yours moving correctly to counter his. If you fail to do this right, all you'll do is ride him further up your chest until either his crotch or leg is against your chin. From that point on, the only way out is to take a big bite. Now you see why it is better to do it right the first time, guys?

## OTHER ASPECTS OF WRASSLIN'

Now let's cover a few other points here that may surprise you. The first surprise is that the chapter on how to break holds covered most of the information you need to do well against your opponent's attacks while you're both on the floor. The back twist gives you the action you need for a draw. The forward twist is the action for punching out of a grip. The forward twist is also what you need to drive any of his punches into the ground. Elbow near your hip, fist near your face, arm snapping down, and a fast forward twist will block the most powerful punch he can throw while on the ground. If he starts hooking you in the short ribs, same thing but with a back twist. Of course, you can do more to mess up a punch by placing your hand on his shoulder or elbow than a whole messa blocks. Once there, just push it another direction.

I've had people ask me what my secret is for wrestling, usually after we've had a playful tussle and they've had the shit surprised out of them. You'd think that weight and muscle would have a lot to do with it. Not necessarily.

In fact, what I base my wrestling on is the snake. Most people think of their arms as clubs—punches, swings, etc. All those movements can be seen like a giant fixed stick. However if you've ever had a snake slither around your arm, you know another type of movement. A snake will coil and wrap itself around your arm depending on where it wants to go. So imagine your hand as a snake's head and your forearm as the snake's body. From there, slither around until you get to a direction you want to go. Then, like a snake striking at a bird in a tree, dart suddenly in that direction.

It sounds like a weird way to describe it, but you'd be amazed at not only how much more mobility you can get in your arms but how much power is involved when you straighten out your arm. What you have to do to make this easier is let your elbow roll down and up. Twirl your wrist to let the snake's head go in whatever direction it wants. The move shown in the photos on the next page is amazingly effective.

All I'm doing there is allowing the snake's head (my hand) to slither around his elbow. That sets up the leverage that I need to snap his arm away. When I straighten my arm out, the *whip* is blowing his arm away, not the pressure of my muscles pushing his arm.

Another key point to wrestling is not locking your elbows. I'm not only talking straight out where they can get broken, but even on an angle. If I have my elbow locked in a 90 degree turn, if someone presses on my forearm, my entire arm will move. If however, I have snake arms, if he pushes against my forearms and I suddenly relax enough to let him slide off, he has a serious opening in his defenses. That's because his arm is now sticking way the hell out

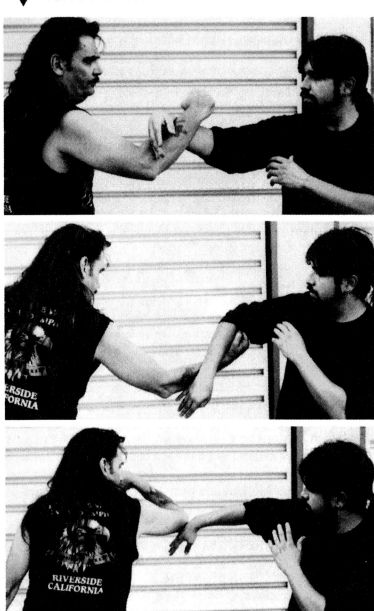

*Snake arms.*

there. Ever been in a tug of war where your opponent suddenly let's go? Same thing; his energy, which was pushing against you, suddenly doesn't have anything stopping it. He goes flying off into left field. In the meantime, you slip out of the way and then snap back.

While I've pictured these moves standing up, they most definitely work while landing on the ground. Play around with them and see how. In fact, for about a month, I would recommend you and your friends get together and practice wrasslin'. I'm not bullshitting you when I tell you that'll put you about a month ahead of everyone else.

• • • • • •

I've pretty well given you the basics for street wrestling. While there are a few moves for snapping arms, they're a little more advanced. (You really have to be able to move well in the forward twist. The other thing is the guy has to lock his arm out straight. Rare occurrence on the ground.)

I would assume by this time that you know better than to let him get on top of you. That curled leg and bottom arm of yours are the best tools you have to prevent that from happening. When he tries to get too close, scoot away when you can. If he tries to climb on top of you, do the launch I showed you earlier to get him away from you.

Again, the most important thing is not to stay down there. Hurt him hard and fast, and break free when he recoils in pain. Even with practice, most of the moves available won't end a fight right then and there. That's cool, as you are only getting him to let go of you. That's because he's discovered the hard way that holding onto you hurts too damn much.

Don't go for the holds or arm locks. Nelsons (full or half), pins, and other fun techniques don't wash out there in Boomtown. You cannot afford the luxury of being on the ground when there are other people present. The next chapter will seriously drive that point home.

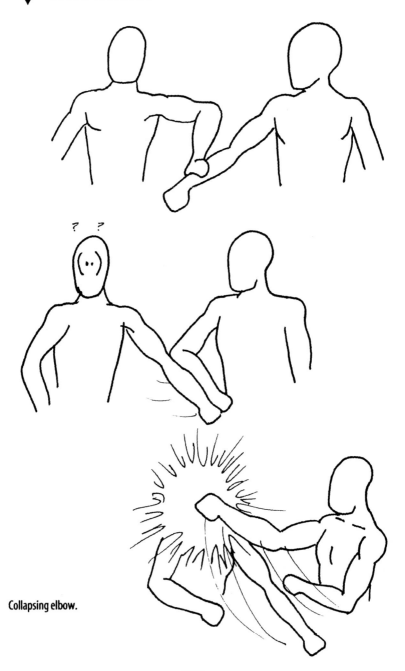

Collapsing elbow.

## FOOTNOTES

[1] I have to admit, I wimp out at anything over 30 feet and over a 5.6. From those points on, I use ropes. Even I will only push it so far.

[2] I ran into a guy in a bookstore who was commenting on *Pool Cues, Beer Bottles, and Baseball Bats.* He's right. It's a technical breakdown of how to use various basic categories of weapons. Westerners understand the principles of physics better than anyone else in the world. It's the math that makes it confusing. Even if you don't think you understand physics, you'd be amazed at how much general knowledge you have about the subject. I'm lousy at math, but I got a good grip on what hurts and why it does.

[3] I've heard these called a swing, loop punch, or shovel punch. It's what most people consider a hook, but it's actually a swinging, looping, wide punch that is incredibly inefficient anyway. While it's a bozo move on your feet, it's a serious jerk-off while on the ground.

[4] I cover many key aspects of how to hold hands and how to place them into tender spots of the anatomy in my book, *Fists, Wits, and a Wicked Right.* While it may sound like I'm trying to peddle my books, a whole lot of what I've had to do is break down all this knowledge into different areas. Unless I wanted to make a huge book the size of an unabridged dictionary, this fragmentation is necessary to focus on certain areas. The problem is that related information ends up in other books. Sorry . . .

[5] These guys also do things like carry a pocketful of ground pepper and iron shavings to toss into people's eyes.

[6] The way most people try to strangle someone is with one hand on top of the other. Hence you end up with an overhand and an underhand.

[7] Also, while I believe the risk of getting AIDS is overblown, I would seriously recommend care if you end up in a fight in jail or the slums.

⁸ Use the same bottle of mouthwash that you kept in your glove compartment before you discovered that mouthwash just ups the alcohol content of your Breathalyzer test.

⁹ Most of the Chinese forms have major investments in these types of techniques. Tiger, Leopard, Mantis, Snake—all of them have moves designed to rip muscles from their placement. So when you hear an impact fighter (karate, taekwon do, etc.) bad mouthing the Chinese styles because they "get their asses kicked" in tournaments, know that A) these are not taught to Americans by most Chinese instructors, and B) even if they were, they wouldn't be allowed in tournaments. In live-fire application, Chinese forms are much nastier.

¹⁰ Or a forward arch if the guy is behind you. The back of the head is just as effective. My snoring proves it.

# 6 ▼ NOT ONLY CAN YOU KEEP A GOOD MAN DOWN, BUT YOU DAMN WELL BETTER!

*"Rise and look around you."*
—Robert Anton Wilson

I got a bro whose last fight exemplifies something that's real important. It was at a time where he was getting sick and tired of "the life." Prior to that he had been one of the baddest motherfuckers around. I'm talking a personal body count in the hundreds, no lie. (One of the key points between a vet and a punk is a punk will look at you and wonder if he can take you. A vet will look at you and decide how he'd take you out.) Nearly 15 years after this incident took place, I met this man and even then decided that the only safe way to do him would be through cross hairs. I've mentioned before that becoming a bad ass is the easy part; it's easing off the throttle that will kill you. Well, he was right in the middle of trying to ease off.

Anyway, my bro was walking down the street and this guy was mouthin' at him. Until you get there, it is impossible to describe how fucking tired of fighting you can get. My bro was there, which explains why he didn't follow procedure. He was trying to walk away (which was a big enough break in tradition by itself), but this guy wasn't going to let it go. Finally, mi hermano slowed down and let the guy catch up. He threw what he calls the "sucker punch of my career." He caught the guy square and sent him down like a ton of lead. Remember, this is a man who survived three tours in Vietnam, the military bar district of Japan, and Cass Corridor in Detroit. That he dropped the guy with a sucker punch was as unusual as the sun coming up.

As the guy was lying there, my bro looked at him and said, "Whaddya think of that motherfucker?" The guy shook his head and got back up. Mi hermano's generosity resulted in him seriously bruising that guy's hands with his face. Even now, after all these years he still can't believe he let that guy get up.

My bro knew better than to let a guy get up. The same man who'd casually kicked God knows how many people let the last one get up. When he was in it deep, his motto was "you go down and stay down." You can bet that up until that moment, he practiced what he preached. But he was "tired." When you're tired, you make mistakes. Fortunately, this one didn't get him killed. You have to understand, if the guy was pissed before, getting knocked onto his ass is going to make him worse than a badger with a toothache when he gets up. All too often, if someone goes down, when he comes up it's with a weapon in his hand. This is what I mean when I say mistakes like this can kill you.

Now I also gotta cop to having blown it on this issue myself. The last time I got kicked in the balls by a black belt, I not only let him get up, I also tried to break up a fight during the hot period. The owner of the company, a woman who hated violence but loved what beer sales were in 105-degree heat, was standing right there. When I showed up, one guy was on the ground and the other guy was standing over him. My personal preference would have been to knock the other dude down too . . . from behind. However, it was a known fact that if I had landed a full-blown blitzkrieg on these guys in front of her, I would have been blackballed in a hot New York second. I fucking knew better! Nonetheless, I had to walk right into the middle of it and try to maintain the peace. Fortunately, the owner couldn't really argue as to the need for violence after I got kicked in the nuts.[1]

Now let's look at this basic rule of fighting: "If he goes down, don't let him get back up!" Floor fighting is probably one of the most brutal forms of combat. This is because it is also one of the most desperate. I can't begin to tell you the risks you face if you let your opponent get back up. Once it hits the floor, fighting goes up a level, no matter what the situation is. If you go down alone, it's more dangerous. If you go down together, it's more fierce. If you knock him down, he's going to be flamed and wanting to hurt you if he gets up.

One thing that amazes the shit out of me is the number of people who you can knock on their ass and they still don't get it, especially if you do it with some sort of judo move or throw. My partner Tup and I once ran on a Code 3 knife incident. We had been listening to trouble develop when we heard, "KNIFE! CODE 3!" from the head of the night security (a grizzled old biker) just before his radio went dead. We showed up, but our boss already had this guy sitting down with his legs out in front of him. He was kneeling on his legs and had the guy in a headlock. This guy was vainly trying to punch, but when someone's got you curled up and tucked under his arm, you're not going to be doing any effective punching. I would have to give this a 9.5 on the "proscribed takedown" scale.[2] What cracked us up was that the guy was sitting there in a reverse chokehold saying, "Let me up motherfucker! I'll kick your ass!"

Let me tell you, it was hard not to laugh. This guy had just had his knife ripped from his hand, been knocked on his ass, and was inches away from being "choked out," but still he was going to "kick ass." Not this time, pal. It's at times like this that you realize that, by definition, half of the population is of below-average intelligence. The problem with proscribed takedowns and nicey-nice throws is there is no "attitude interruption."

If there is a problem with throwing styles, this is it. If you throw someone in a gentle and controlled manner, there is nothing to interrupt his attitude. He has no reason to stay on the ground and behave. The same thing about an arm lock—he's going to get more pissed off if you just hold him at the edge of pain. Here is where my professional ethics clashed with my street sense. What happens all too often is if you drop someone too easily, he doesn't realize that he has been thrown by a superior fighter. He just thinks he fell on his ass, and this pisses him off more. The same thing happens, I should point out, if you either dodge or merely block someone's attacks.[3] If someone is in attack mode, he needs some sort of incoming information that is louder than his attitude. This is what I call an attitude interrupter.

If you don't do this, nine times out of ten the guy will just get more and more pissed. If you have the guy in a hold, you're going to have to hold him until he cools down or until enough backup arrives so you all can fall on him once you let him go. This whole situation is complicated by his friends. While you may have been quick enough to tell them to back off or you'll snap his arm or neck, all too often if they see you drop someone in a hold, they'll jump in to save him. Now you have multiple attackers, one of which is infuriated that you held him. I hope you have Blue Cross.

I have seen the need for attitude interrupters again and again. In fact I would say about 60 percent of the time, just throwing someone or dropping him into a hold will only piss him off more. If, on the other hand, you give him an attitude interrupter, you often can reopen negotiations. If, for instance, you can get the information across to him that as long as he is on the floor he's a noncombatant, he might choose to reconsider getting up. "*Stay down*" as a warning works really well, especially if it is delivered a few seconds after a kick to the face. Let him realize that the only way he'll get more punishment is if he tries to get back up.

If you don't give the guy an incentive to stay on the floor, he's just going to pop right back up and try to fight again. When I say my favorite move is to knock someone's feet out from under him, that means that not only is the guy going to hit the ground hard, but I'm going to lay one or two good ones into his short ribs. That means his attitude has to overcome not only his body slamming into the ground but a few swift kicks to his ribs.

You have to remember that there is a difference between a fight and combat. A fight is to establish dominance. Generally, the fight goes only until everyone knows whose dick is bigger. Weird dynamics here, folks. You have to be aware of where you are and what the rules are. What works in one circle will get a bottle broken over your head in another. I don't know where you are, so I can't give you a hard and fast rule, because the rules change depending on your location. Generally, if an altercation is a pissing contest or you're dealing with an obnoxious drunk, my recommendation is to knock the guy down and interrupt his attitude. Don't attack beyond that, but let him know that if he tries to get up, you'll seriously hurt him. Often if you don't press your advantage, his friends won't jump in, but if there ever was a situation-by-situation call, this is it. If he still tries to get up, you nail his ass while he's got his body weight committed.

If, on the other hand, it is a serious brawl where you need to make sure he doesn't get back up, you come in hard and fast and maul him while he's down. Either he breaks something on his way down or you slam your boots into his side a few times before you turn your attention to the other guests. My recommendation is to start using this type of fighting any place where there is the serious possibility of weapons or group stompings.

Understand that you have just been given a structure in which you can operate. The idea behind boundaries is to keep a system going. What you as an experienced fighter have to contend with is the likelihood of there being further complications in your life. If you miscall the situation and go ballistic on someone that you shouldn't have, or you run into a sniveler (a guy who starts shit, then runs to the police and courts when he loses), you're going to be in a heap of shit. I'm talking jail, prison, and civil suits here.

If you make it so witnesses say that you tried to prevent the fight from escalating, it's going to go in your favor. (Of course if you're in the military and you get caught brawling, your ass is in the sling no matter who started it.) A guy who gets up after you've not only knocked him down but told him not to get up is not going to convince anyone that he didn't want to continue the fight. Still, even if you win a court case, it's going to take a long time and be very expensive.[4]

Here is another one of my famous "officially I didn't tell you this" bits of information. What I used to do was tell people that I had taken down that if I ever saw them again (if that was possible) or if they went to the police, I'd kill them. On the street there is a definite likelihood that if someone tells you that, he is serious. Many a court case has been dropped by the person pressing charges taking a trip to the morgue. Also, this move is not the move of an amateur. It's like you calling a guy on his hands slipping out of sight—this carries the message to the guy that you've been around. Of course, you have to be convincing when you say it to the person.

Now, I always settled for this little technique, but a partner of mine used to do one better. He'd take their driver's license. He wouldn't take any money, just the license. Furthermore, he'd make sure they saw him look at the name and address and then straight at them. You know when someone threatens you in that situation that you're in deep shit if you snivel. The guy knows where you live. My friend's contention was even if he got stopped, all he could be charged with was petty theft. In the meantime, the message was clear to the guy he left on the floor.

The point I'm trying to make here is that if you have

some form of operating structure, you're not adrift in these waters. Just because you have an operating structure, however, does not mean the other guy does. If you hit the floor, unless the guy otherwise proves it by telling you your safety depends on your sitting there and behaving, assume that he will try to press his advantage! That means he not only will kick you when you're down, he might not stop either. His friends may want to join in the fun. This is called a stomping, and it is bad news. I know a guy who was in the hospital for eight weeks after a stomping. Not only was he in a total body cast, but he had internal injuries. Most nonweapon homicides occur during this point. *You don't want to get stomped!* And the best way not to get stomped is get off the floor.

There are two good ways to get off the floor quickly. One is to turn your fall into a roll and use that energy to bounce back up. The other way is to use your legs as a compressed spring. It may not come as a surprise to you, but you can combine these two very well.

Stone cold, flat out, and simple, what you do not want to do is get up normally. Most people get up from the floor by doing a push-up that raises their torso. They then proceed to walk their legs under them. Once this occurs, all of their weight is committed to all fours. That's too many "alls." The term "sitting duck" in no way begins to describe this situation. Once the person is in this position, he leans back and then relies on his legs to lift him up. If you want to break this down, it is a five-step process: 1) position onto stomach, 2) push up, 3) walk in, 4) lean back/straighten body, and 5) stand up. Do you want to know how much fucking damage I can do in the time it takes to do a five-step process?!

While each point is rife with danger, it is that damn four-point committed body weight where the shit can come down the worst. If you have your weight committed, there is no way you'll be able to block any attack that comes in, bottom line. Any attack to the head/face or lower rib cage/kidney is going to land. Until you've taken a solid kidney shot, you cannot imagine how much it can hurt. It'll drop you like a sack of potatoes if the guy has had a chance to wind up. A kick to the floating ribs will not only break ribs but knock your breath out. A blow to the head with a tool will often cause unconsciousness, vomiting, brain damage, comas, and sometimes death. A full strike to the face means a broken jaw, knocked-out teeth, wrenched neck, broken cheek bones, and occasionally unconsciousness. If the guy is behind you, he can try to kick a field goal with your nuts.

Normal way of getting up.

These are all things that you do not want to happen to you. However, if you've told your opponent to stay down and he tries to get up, there are your options. Practice low hard kicks with the shins. Muay Thai has got some of the nastiest shin kicks around. Believe it or not, in many cases your shin will transfer impact better than your foot. The kick is like a short "stick kick" with the leg locked and the hips powering it with body weight. These work extremely well with body shots. (Snap kicks work

well with the head and face.) Remember, when you tell the guy to stay down, you are in position to kick. That leg is cocked back and ready to fire at the first sign of rebellion. If you're standing there in a superman pose, he might be able to move before you can kick.

I've also seen people lever themselves off their arms. They straighten their arms and then roll their body forward. This forward roll puts their feet back under them and they spring forward. If you're standing there in front of them in a heroic stance, you're about to get tackled. On the other hand if you're cocked and ready, your attacker is about to throw himself into a front snap kick. If you're the one on the ground, before you consider this move make sure he doesn't have one waiting in the wings.

Levering off of arms to get up.

181

Now these are the two most common ways for someone to get up. While the second one is faster, I don't recommend it because it usually results in you being on the floor again. This time with company, but you're still back on the floor. Both of these moves are susceptible to kicks, too. So before you consider getting up, *make sure that you've bought distance from your opponent or stunned him enough that he isn't going to attack while you're getting up!* If you've bought distance before getting up, who cares if he attacks; by the time he gets to where you are, you're back on two feet!

A quick spring back to your feet is critical to getting off the floor safely. You have to minimize the time that you're vulnerable. The key point to springing up is getting a bent limb underneath you. Once you have that, you can piston with that limb.

People often ask me how to draw a knife quickly. I have to tell them that the most critical element for success is positioning the knife. It's the same thing with regaining your feet. The critical element for getting up quickly is getting your legs underneath your body but in such a way that when they straighten out they will sky rocket you back up. It doesn't matter if it's one leg or two, just so long as you can push up. Look at these positions in the photos on page 183.

As well as the fact that each of these positions has at least one leg that, by straightening, will shoot me back to a standing position, what else do they have in common? Think about it while I tell you something else.

Each of these positions is easily attainable by rolling and twisting. Go out onto a padded surface or lawn and practice rolling and twisting into these positions from the ground. Imagine an attacker at a certain point and roll away from him and into something like these positions. A curled limb, whether arm or leg, will give you the extra spring you need to get there.

The most difficult roll to accomplish is sideways. This is if your attacker is to the side and you're laid out lengthwise.

*Potential
standing
positions.*

In this case you have to roll away from him. While rolling you have to curl your legs up to your chest. When you revolve around to your front again, you have to push off with your arms in a diagonal direction to get into your pre-stand position. Then you straighten up.

One thing you have to understand is *you have to practice these moves!* This is not only so you know how to do them instinctively, hence faster, but so you know what muscles you need to build up. No muscles, no get up fast. Simple as that. This is something else you need to practice while your practicing the tumbles and rolls that I mentioned in Chapter 2. If you have well-developed leg muscles (like from bike riding, rock climbing, tennis, martial art training, or swimming), you can rocket back up to your feet before he can close the distance.

Now the answer to the trivia question I asked earlier. In every one of those positions, my arms are free. I do not have my body weight committed on them when I am in a vulnerable position. Even though I am in a dangerous position, it it made less dangerous by my conforming to the third law of floor fighting—regroup your defensive/ offensive capabilities immediately.

Even if the sucker attacks before I get my wobbly ass up, I can hold off his attacks using the triangle. I can't take full impact in that position, but you can bet your dick I can counter his attacks!

## FOOTNOTES

[1] It was 20 minutes later, as we were filling out the incident report in base, that I looked at my boss and said, "I just realized something."

"What?"

"I just got kicked in the balls. I'm going off into a corner and whimper for awhile."

The fact that I discovered that I had gotten to a point where I could take a crotch shot and sheer fury would keep me up and fighting still didn't make up for the pain.

[2] "Proscribed takedowns" are the authorized, nondamaging, let's-not-get-sued-or-accused-of-brutality restraining holds that are used by police, prison guards, mental health workers, and any other professionals along those lines. They are not as effective as many other moves because they are designed to not seriously damage the person they are being applied to. Of course, the people who are attacking have no such restrictions. Prisoners, street scum, and wackos are real happy to do violence to you, but they will sue if you fight back.

Not too long ago, I saw a mother trying to sue the man who shot her two sons while they tried to rob his jewelry store. He'd taken lead in the exchange, but he killed them. There she was on TV, whining and bitching that she'd lost her children. This is the mentality that has led to proscribed takedowns being necessary for a company to survive. Now you know why, if you're a bouncer and you quell a fight, you are often fired. The owner is protecting himself from a suit.

[3] My last personal fight, as opposed to conflicts in the line of duty or helping someone else out, was along these lines. The guy attacked me and was throwing punches and kicks that I was swatting away. As I was blocking, I was telling him I didn't want to fight him. I was trying to calm him down. Instead of realizing that all those blocks and my talking while he was attacking ferociously meant that I was a better fighter than he was, he got more and more angry that his attacks weren't landing. Finally, I stopped blocking and fired off a snap kick to his nuts. Later, I heard he had to go to the emergency room for blood clots.

[4] By the way, it's not a bad idea to have done your homework early. Go out now and find both a good criminal and civil lawyer— criminal for the problems with the cops and civil for being sued. You don't have to pay the guy a retainer if you don't want to, although that helps. Just having a good lawyer's name and number before trouble starts saves you all kinds of hassles if it does.

# NOW THAT THE DANCE IS OVER

*"It's your blood."*
—One of the best attitude adjusters I've heard

I was sitting in a coffee shop with my bro. In between the times when we were playing with the toaster that the restaurant had put on our table, we were having a conversation. As I did a slap block to knock the oversized bread down into the toaster, he looked at me and said, "Man, I gotta hand it to you about writing this book. I could see maybe four or five pages. But after that, what is there to say?"

While we were trying to dig the same piece of toast out of the toaster, I began to question him about what he knew about floor fighting. After 10 or so minutes of him answering some pretty technical questions, he realized that not only was there more to floor fighting than he originally thought, but he knew a whole lot more about the subject than he thought he did. I should mention that during this conversation, I was nearly fatally wounded by a piece of flying toast.

What I have done with this book is try to cover the subject from the time that you start to go down to when you are back on your feet. When I originally came up with the idea for this book, I was trying to figure out how to organize it. I had originally intended for it to be in two parts—you down/him up and both down. Ah well, the best laid plans of mice and men . . . As I began to write it, however, the book began to take on the aspect of a pin ball bouncing back and forth as it heads down the field. This actually makes more sense to me because, the truth be told, you don't know how the situation is going to develop. In a fight you can be absolutely convinced it's going one way, and the next thing you know it's going in an altogether different direction. You have to be able to adapt at a moment's notice.

It really is incredibly important to know how to handle yourself on the ground. I've seen an incredible number of fights end up on the floor, and I've seen many good fighters go down and stay down because they didn't know the things I've told you about in this book. I've always wondered why nobody really paid much attention to floor fighting, especially formal martial arts. It's sort of like ignoring the shark fin in the pool, if you ask me.

Go out and grab your friends and practice what you've read in this book (make nice on the maimers and gouges, though). All the books in the world are nowhere as good as actual free-form practice. It is critical that you know where you don't want to go—not only what that territory feels like, but what the borders that mean you're heading in there feel like. Even if you do it only for a month, you'll pick up important knowledge that can save your ass in a real brawl.

Take care out there.

Animal